AT DELHI

AT DELHI

LOVAT FRASER

GYAN

Published by

Gyan Publishing House
5, Ansari Road
Daryaganj, New Delhi-110002
Phone: 011-47034999, 9811692060
E-mail: books@gyanbooks.com

Distribution Network
gyanbooks.com
India, USA, Canada, UK, Australia, France

ISBN: 978-81-212-8927-6 (PB)
First Published, 1903

2nd Impression 2023

Printed at: Gyan Press, Delhi.

AT DELHI

AUTHOR: LOVAT FRASER

AT DELHI

AT DELHI

BY

LOVAT FRASER

BOMBAY:
THE "TIMES OF INDIA" PRESS, and THACKER & CO. LD.

LONDON:
THE "TIMES OF INDIA" OFFICE, 121, FLEET ST., E.C.
and
W. THACKER & CO., 2, CREED LANE, LUDGATE HILL, E.C.

"Hear the long waves of acclamation roll!"

To T. J. B.

PREFACE.

THIS volume contains selections from the narratives which appeared in the *Times of India* during the recent Coronation Assemblage at Delhi. The chronicle was written for the most part at the end of the telegraph wire, without any thought of republication in book form. It was only after the issues containing the principal messages ran out of print, that the proposal to issue some of them in a more permanent shape was made. The accounts of certain of the gatherings, including the Opening of the Art Exhibition, the State Service, the Assault-at-Arms, and the Small Investiture at the Viceregal Party on January 9th, are omitted, as well as a number of sketches of scenes in the camps and the city. Even as it is, I fear that a series of descriptions of pageantry which were meant to be perused singly, may when read in bulk be found rather cloying.

The chapters entitled "India's Bazaar," "An Off Day," and "Princes of India," are from the pen of my colleague, Mr. L. Elwin Neame, whose initials are attached to each.

The note about the Taj is added by way of tailpiece.

Acknowledgments are due to the Proprietors of the *Times of India* for permission to republish these contributions to their journal.

L. F.

BOMBAY, *February* 5, 1903.

CONTENTS.

AT DELHI.

I.

THE ROAD THITHER.

December 11.

ONE hears alarming things about the vicissitudes of a journey to Delhi just now. I can only speak of my own experience. I travelled by the express which left Bombay at four o'clock on Tuesday afternoon. We were due at Delhi last night at midnight, and arrived only fifty minutes late. Those fifty minutes were lost during the last twenty miles. Throughout the whole of the run on the Great Indian Peninsula Railway and Indian Midland Railway to Tundla, we were almost invariably punctual. If we lost a few minutes on one section, we made it up on the next. The stories told about the interminable delays appear to relate almost exclusively to the East Indian Railway, which is undoubtedly becoming more muddled every day. Traffic from the Bombay side continues to be handled with promptitude and smartness. If goods get swept into the congested mass that now gluts Ghaziabad Junction, a few miles from Delhi, that is not the fault of the Great Indian

Peninsula Railway. At the same time, it would be unwise to assume that my good fortune may continue to be typical. The authorities are plainly apprehensive of increasing delay as Christmas approaches. The best advice that can be offered to people proposing to attend the Durbar is: Start as soon as you can, unless you are fortunate enough to have a seat in a special train. To consignors of goods one would say: Send your packages off at once if you wish them to arrive at all.

After leaving Bombay, it does not take long to realise that one is moving northward. You reach for your overcoat as the train slowly climbs the Thal Ghaut in the gathering twilight, and when you turn in for the night, you see to it that there are not too many open windows in the carriage. Next morning you waken to find that you are passing through the thick jungles of the Vindhya Range, and have reached a climate where beer off the ice ceases to be a joy. The people on the wayside platforms are swathed in blankets and shawls, and look as miserable as the Hindu usually contrives to appear in chilly weather. All day long the monotonous plains of Central India are traversed. They are dreary enough now, while still green after the late rains; but one rather wishes that the troops of visitors from England might have to cross them once during the torrid desolation of May. In the course of the morning Bina is reached; and the sole discernible attraction about Bina is that it is the place where you breakfast. Then on until the shadows begin to lengthen, past the great grim fort of Jhansi; past Gwalior, set in the midst of leafy groves, on a plain dominated by a fort-crowned hill; past many a little nameless stronghold, whose narrow loopholes tell of the days of strife before peace settled upon the land. Last and best scene of all, in the misty sunset, a glimpse of a river, gleaming red far away to the point where its waters merge with the advancing darkness.

Presently the train steams past mighty battlemented walls, and pulls up in a station blazing with light and thronged with people. It is Agra, but you look in vain as you approach for a glimpse of the Taj. For Agra is bathed in white fog, which even the moonlight fails to pierce; it remains a picture of huge vague structures, with here and there a lamp shining warmly. And the cold grows more intense every hour, until at last, when you plunge into the long tunnel-like station at Tundla, where the fog lingers and the air is absolutely biting, you feel that this place is not the India you know; it is the Underground Railway on a November night.

From Tundla onwards the pace is slower, and there are frequent stoppages. You drowsily wonder whether the engine is affected by the still falling thermometer. By this time even the expedient of closing every window fails to exclude the all-pervading chilliness; even inanimate steel, you think, must feel the temperature. Finally, there is a faint peep of a broad river bed, more fortifications loom before you, and you alight in another great station a few minutes before one. The first feeling is one of intense surprise. Where are the mountains of luggage, the pyramids of packages piled from floor to ceiling, the babel and the inextricable confusion, of which you have read so much? The platform is as clear as a billiard table, and only a few porters are visible. The parcel office contains just the ordinary collection of boxes and bundles neatly packed on racks, but with ample room for more. Upon a table is a huddled heap covered by a blanket. You lift the blanket, and reveal a solitary clerk, who may be sleeping the sleep of the overworked, but does not look it. You see your baggage packed upon a tonga, and are driving along the roads of Imperial Delhi in a few minutes. There is no noise, no confusion, and certainly no visible muddle. So far as that placid and orderly station was concerned, there might have been no Durbar toward at all. I write of things as I found them. Yet honest gentlemen, whose word may be relied on, assure me that a few hours before I arrived, the station was still in the appalling condition described with strict accuracy in your columns last Monday.* And there is a clue to the marvellous transformation. It is said that Some One sent a Telegram ; and then, in the mysterious way things happen in India, the

* The station again relapsed into confusion a day or two afterwards, and remained in a muddle until the middle of January.

whole place was cleared. If this be true, one wonders why Some One does not send one of these wonder-working Telegrams to Ghaziabad; for rumour declares that there are nine hundred trucks full of goods at that bewildered junction, and that they seem likely to stay there.

The Delhi tongas are in notable contrast with the Bombay hackney carriages in point of speed. You are rattled along at a rapid pace, which becomes almost embarrassing when you suddenly collide with an electric lamp post and your baggage is pitched out on the road. The installation of the electric light in the city seems a little belated. The posts are there, in the very middle of the thoroughfare, as you ruefully discover if one of their warning lanterns gets blown out; but Delhi still awaits the discerning beams of the new illuminant. You drive along a road or two, where there are houses, and then emerge upon dim, open tree-clad spaces. There is nothing to be seen, and if there were you would not care. The present writer once arrived in Venice at three o'clock on a freezing December morning. That was, despite the weather, a novel and unforgettable experience. But Delhi in the small hours in December! B-r-r-r! The only thing you are conscious of is the cold. For a moment the mind is roused to other things when you notice the shadowy outline of rising ground on your right. Can that little slope be the famous Ridge, you ask yourself. But daylight will serve to answer that question, and in the meantime you are wishing that you owned all the blankets Witney ever produced. Another half-mile and you are suddenly aware of great arc lights, shining amid a perfect wilderness of tents. You plunge into the maze. You enter a tent flooded with the electric light. Delhi can wait until the dawn. But here, at least, are the blankets.

II.

TRAVELS IN CAMP.

December 12.

THERE is no commanding eminence from which to survey the whole of the Durbar Camp. The Ridge is not lofty enough, and if it were the morning haze and the afternoon dust would limit the view. To see the Canvas City which has arisen on the plain outside the walls of Delhi, it is necessary to travel through it and gaze upon it in sections. The newcomer, having first stuck his head outside his tent to make quite sure that the morning sun is really above the horizon, sallies forth with the ingenuous idea of "riding round the camp"; and it is not until you have absolutely lost yourself amid a wilderness of tents that you realise what you have undertaken. You plough your way along a road deep in sand, with plenty of big flints scattered about to give variety to the surface. The fifty miles of new roads, by the way, are at present of very varying quality. There will be a mile of road in faultless condition, at the end of which you find yourself embedded in a sand bank. You drag through that and turn a corner, to be confronted by a rope, the legend "Road Closed," and in the middle distance a stray steam-roller. But every one says it will be "all right by the First"—if it does not rain.

On all sides are tents, big and little, round and square, from the lordly marquee to the tiny gipsy tents where the servants shelter. There cannot have been such a collection since the tent-dwellers of Central Asia set out to conquer the world. No other country could furnish a like spectacle. It is worth coming to Delhi to see the tents alone. Many have mud fire-places neatly let into the walls, while without rise square chimneys of white-washed mud. Over the sea of white roofs a flag-staff appears, with the Union Jack hanging limply in the still morning air. It marks the Commander-in-Chief's quarters, and his Excellency is evidently in residence. You turn into a broad well-kept road, and emerge upon a large open space surrounded by spacious dwellings. A circular drive before the biggest marquee encloses a plot of grass, with flower-beds. The happy idea of bedecking Lord Kitchener's camp with flowers has been ruined by the dust. The plants are dirty and dejected, the blossoms are begrimed. Elsewhere a forlorn coolie had actually been set to dust a bed of flowers with a red feather dusting-brush!

You make your way up an adjacent gentle slope to the Viceregal House, a not very imposing structure of khaki colour, relieved by white pillars and cornices. In front, the outlook is neat and smooth enough, but the ground behind is an unkempt desert of sands and boulders. The terrace is littered with furniture not yet unpacked. Standing upon it, you look past the magnificent collection of tents where the Duke and Duchess of Connaught and their suite will be housed, down a long vista of roadway to the distant polo grounds. Wandering along this road, you stray presently into the camp of the Governor of Bombay. It seems the most trim and orderly camp of all, without a trace of slovenliness to offend the eye. The tents are ranged around a huge oblong lawn, green and refreshing after the sand and dust without. The designers have wisely refrained from disfiguring it with banks of sickly flowers, though a few dwarf palms are dotted about. Every tent has its fire-place and chimney and boarded floor, and is cosily furnished. People say that Lord Northcote's guests will be more comfortable than any other party in camp, and tell you wonderful stories of billiard tables, and tents with glass doors, and other marvels.

The sun is fairly high now, and you ruefully reflect that you have not got very far on that "ride round the camp." So you press onwards amid the all-encompassing tents, and hurry along a network of roads selected at random. The "light railway" —it is really nothing more than a steam tramway, with carriages very like the Bombay trams—is crossed, and you reach the Alipur Road, one of the few arterial thoroughfares in this rather chaotic place. All the roads are so thronged that it is hard to believe that the official ceremonies are still seventeen days distant. Gangs of melancholy coolies, squads of soldiers, busy camp officials, mounted orderlies, stray postmen and telegraph messengers and chaprassies, pervade the scene. In a bye-road pleasantly shaded with trees, you see a couple of horsemen whom nobody appears to notice. The foremost is quietly dressed in dark tweed, with a grey cloth cap. Only at the moment of passing do you suddenly perceive the face bronzed and reddened by long exposure, the heavy moustache, the cold stern eyes, and realise in a flash that it is Lord Kitchener.

On past the interminable tents, moving ever northward. Surely you must be near the verge of the camp now? You seem to have been riding for hours. At last you emerge upon a wide bare plain. You think: "At any rate I have ridden all along one side of the place." Then a convenient notice board informs you that this particular tract—it looks like a couple of ten acre fields thrown into one—is reserved for the accommodation of the Royal Field Artillery, and you grow a little dubious about the extent of your achievement. An affable stranger passes, and you enquire if you are anywhere near the Amphitheatre. You fancy it should be hard by, but it seems to have coyly concealed itself. He points towards the north-west, and says:—"You see that village over there?"

You select a village so far away that the houses are only indistinctly visible, and ask if that is the one.

"No, not that one. Farther on to the right, where there is a line of white wall on a hillock."

"What, do you mean that place away towards the horizon?"

"Yes. Well, the Amphitheatre is behind that."

And away you pound across rough and broken country, wondering whether the Camp extends from here to Umballa. As a matter of fact, you afterwards find that you have taken a rather circuitous route, and also that the white wall is not quite so far away as it looks: but the point is that all this time you have never left the camp limits. The size of the place, and the distances between one point and another, must be seen to be realised. There is an Exhibition somewhere, goodness knows where; I have not yet set eyes on it.

Weird sounds of music presently assail the ear. They do not resolve themselves into any particular tune, but convey a general impression that about fifty brass bands are somewhere about and have simultaneously gone mad. As you surmount a piece of rising ground the mystery is explained. Here are sections of military bands, dotted about a sort of parade ground, all stolidly engaged in playing tunes, each section cheerfully independent of the others. You remember at last that about two thousand military bandsmen are to play on Durbar Day. At a signal, two or three hundred of them form up two deep, and burst forth into—"The Lost Chord!"

And then you flee towards the Amphitheatre, which finally comes into view. It is an impressive sight, with its roof of creamy white, its cupolas and glittering decorations. It stands in massive solitude on a great dirty-brown plain, far removed from the sights and sounds of the camp. It will seat about ten thousand people. In shape it resembles a horse-shoe, and right opposite the entrance is the Viceroy's dais, projected forward into the arena, and surmounted by a cupola. The troops will be drawn up on the plain outside, facing the Amphitheatre, but only those directly before the entrance will be visible to the spectators. Somehow one feels, standing in the middle of the vast empty arena, that though the Durbar may be the most dramatic and impressive incident of this historic gathering, it will not be the most picturesque. The proportions are too great to be effectually visualised. Then, again, the roof which covers the seats will throw a large proportion of the spectators into deep shadow, and so much of the rich colouring will be lost. Moreover, there is something about Delhi in winter which does not accord with one's traditional ideas of Oriental splendour. Elephants alone do not make an Eastern pageant. We want palm trees and the luxuriant green of the tropics, and above all, warmth. And here in January, even at noontide, the dominant note seems likely to be imparted by the steel-blue wintry sky.

III.

THE DUST OF WAR.

December 13.

THERE was a lull in the campaign. An armistice had been declared to enable the two Armies to concentrate in fresh country, before commencing the second phase of their operations. The Southern Army had passed through the suburbs of Delhi on the previous day, and were now reported to be camped some miles south of the city. One does not often get a chance of seeing twenty thousand of the flower of the Army of India bivouacking under service conditions in the open country, so I determined to go in search of them. It was said that they were to halt for a day's rest just south of the great Mausoleum of Nawab Safdar Jang, one of the numerous tombs that you find scattered about in the midst of seeming desolation for many miles around Delhi. They were therefore on the precise spot where Timur the Tartar and his horde from Samarkand routed the great army of Sultan Mahmud in 1398. Timur gained his victory on December 12th; an army of the first Emperor of all India slept on the battle-ground on the 504th anniversary of that sanguinary encounter; one wonders if anybody noticed the coincidence.

It was bitterly cold when I started off in the pallid dawn, before the sun had hoisted itself above the shoulder of the Ridge. My driver was a man of owlishly vacuous mind, who did not even know the road to the Kutab Minar; but one could scarcely miss a whole Army, one thought. The dismal streets just inside the western wall of Delhi were already astir when we clattered through them. Native quarters in India never present such a scene of unredeemed squalor as at daybreak, before the sunlight has lit up their rich colouring. It was a relief to pass under one of the massive gates of the city, and leave the great walls behind. Needless to say, we had not got a mile beyond the city before the driver expressed blank ignorance of his whereabouts. We pressed onwards by the first road we came to; it might not be the right one, but anyway it led south. A thick haze shut in the view on either side; it was hard to see a couple of hundred yards in any direction; evidently that Army was going to take some finding. Gaunt ruins loomed up at intervals through the mist, for modern Delhi is simply a city set in the midst of the sites of half a dozen other cities abandoned to the lizard and the squirrel. The road was cumbered with creaking carts laden with forage and a medley of furniture. Surely there was no more Durbar Camp here? The Amphitheatre was unknown miles away, to the north of the city.

Yet so it proved; and all along this road were planted, if you please, the camps of the Bombay

Chiefs. They seemed to extend for about a couple of miles. The Chiefs have some long journeys before them if they mean to attend every function of the first few days of January; but they will have the satisfaction of knowing that the camps are in an open and healthy situation. At the very last camp I met a friendly Englishman, who said that the Southern Army had bivouacked the previous night two or three miles to the eastward. A cross-cut put me on the right route at last. Here were waggons loaded with barrels of beer. Clearly the Army could not be very far away. Then came a plain where wreaths of smoke from the embers of countless fires were mingling with the fog. A few natives could be faintly descried beating out the ashes with sticks; but the entire Army, horse, foot, artillery, and baggage train, had vanished into the unknown. Nothing but the smouldering fragments told that they had ever been there. Twenty thousand men marching light, leave astonishingly few traces behind them.

As I turned disappointedly towards Delhi, I was overtaken by a squadron of the Central India Horse; and then I began to realise what marching through dust was like. Instantly the scene became almost invisible. We moved through dense choking clouds. A thick flour settled on clothes and carriage. One heard the clatter of hoofs, the jingling of arms, the hoarse cries of the sowars; but all that could be seen were stray glimpses of a fluttering lance-pennon, of a phantom bearded face, of the white eyeballs of straining horses. Phew! The dust turned the hair a dingy white, and caked in nostrils and throat. Will it be like this on Durbar Day? And what will become of the ladies' dresses? Anyway, let us get out of it. I turned into the fields. More ruins. Some one seemed to have been reproducing the Coliseum in miniature across the plain. On drawing near, it was realized that these two round buildings with tiers of arches must be the remains of the famous Observatory of Raja Jai Singh of Jeypore. Hard by was a huge sundial in brick, perhaps fifty feet high, with steps leading to the apex. I climbed to the top, and gazed towards Delhi. It was clearer now, but there seemed to be an uncommon amount of dust rising along the road as far as one could see. Presently, through the trees that lined the road, the head of a great cavalry column was discernible. I had struck another Army.

There was not much chance of getting back to Delhi after that. This was the First Division of the Northern Army, so a stray officer of the Guides Cavalry said. The rear of the column was miles behind. When a Division marches, it wants the whole road. No one would seek to dispute possession with it in any case, for it is no joke to travel amid the dust of an army. First came a cavalry brigade, mostly native cavalry. To see the native cavalryman at his best you want to look at him off the parade ground. These men were riding with the alert, careless ease of the born trooper. Light, keen-eyed, spare, sitting their horses as though they were part of themselves, begrimed with dust, the beard and moustache whitened, the dark eyes curiously roving, they looked the very type of "the horsemen of the future." What might they not have done in South Africa, had it been deemed possible to pit them against our whilom foes? Then came a couple of companies of the Bikanir Camel Corps, their huge mounts looking quaintly unwarlike, but carrying large quantities of stores. The dust grew thicker every moment, as round a corner trotted a couple of field batteries. There may have been an armistice, but this Division was pressing onward as though eager for instant battle. One noticed how smart the officers looked, in spite of the dust; khaki serge is a fine colour for service conditions. Many wore thick covert-coats of the same colour, for the air was still raw. Then a mountain battery or two, and a miscellaneous assortment of details. And then there was a gap and what seemed like a chance of a dash for Delhi.

I had just driven half a mile, when I came upon an inextricable jam of bullock carts, camels, donkeys laden with earth, palanquins, tongas, and a whole mob of shrieking, excited natives, at a bridge over the Jumna Canal. Emerging from a gap between two low houses, there tramped into view the solid ranks of the 2nd Battalion Gordon Highlanders. They were the head of the 1st Infantry Division, and all dreams of tiffin—breakfast had already become an impossibility—vanished.

One could not help admiring the fine free swing with which the Gordons went past. It is all very well to talk about the petted Highland regiments, but you would have to search a long while through the British Army to find a finer battalion than the 2nd Gordons. There did not appear to be a weedy man among them, and the hard work of the present operation has filled them with health and vigour. Somehow the dark tartan kilts did not show the dust as one would have expected. I noticed that all the company officers carried Lee-Metford carbines, but no swords. More Highlanders—the Argyll and Sutherlands—followed, and then a battalion of Rajputs, and another of Baluchis. The block of traffic on either side of the line of route grew denser every minute. Cross-roads met at that point, and it was amusing to see people trying to break through the column. A man on a big camel checked the whole advance by entangling himself amid the ranks of the 15th Sikhs. The little donkey boys tried to drive their charges through an occasional gap, but the donkeys never failed to stand stock still in the very midst of the adventure. Once a haggard wreck of humanity, carried in a dhoolie, cursed his bearers into making the perilous attempt. In their nervousness they selected the moment when a mule battery was passing, and instantly found themselves bumped and shouldered in all directions. The wasted man in the dhoolie—he looked like a drug-taker—shaking with terror, shrieked imprecations on the entire Army and all its ancestors; but he did not get through. Another party, bearing on high two stark and shrouded forms, were more successful; the troops were halted; way was made for the dead.

There seemed no end to the khaki-clad host as it swept along, bronzed, dusty, sweating,—the sun was high now,—most of the men with the fixed, intent, rather vacant look straight ahead, that tells of long marching. And all the time the dust arose, and eyes and nostrils and throat grew gritty with particles. I clambered on a high bank to look for the tail of the column. The troops were marching by the stagnant waters of the canal. As far as the eye could reach, the ranks stretched out until they were lost to view in the dust-clouds. The Welsh Regiment approached, then a ponderous thirty-pounder battery lumbered along, then the 1st South Wales Borderers from Peshawar, then field hospital sections, then more native infantry. The end came at last. We hastily started along the canal bank to get ahead of the traffic that had been so long held up. We did three hundred yards in a canter, and then—right before us came another column, a medley of vehicles of all kinds, of camels and mules and horses, of mounted officers and men on foot, and a whole rabble of camp followers. It was the transport, and an officer at its head volunteered the information that it might be two miles long, but was probably nearer three. I had had enough of it. I shouldered my overcoat, and started to trudge slowly into Delhi. The last I saw of my unlucky conveyance, it was inextricably wedged in the angle of a wall behind a jam of bullock-carts. For aught I know, it may be there now. And the taste of the dust is still in my throat.

IV.

THE BOMBAY CHIEFS.

December 14.

IT is a far cry from the Central Camp, where I happen to reside, to the abodes now being prepared along the Gurgaon Road, to the south of the city, for the ruling Chiefs of the Bombay Presidency. You have to cross a corner of the Ridge, skirt the west wall of Delhi, traverse the populous suburb of Paharganj, and drive for three or four miles on a road several inches deep in dust to inspect all the Bombay Camps. Yet the Bombay Chiefs, if they did but know it, are in some respects a good deal better off than their compeers from other parts of India. It is true that they are rather isolated, and that they will have an unconscionable distance to go to the Durbar and the two Reviews. On the other hand, they are in an excellent position for attending the State Entry, and the two great functions, the Investiture and the State Ball, which are to be held in the fort. To these ceremonies they will have ready access, and a road all to themselves.

I started this morning to inspect their camps, in the cheerful belief that there would be no difficulty in getting there. We had scarcely got into the main road, when we found ourselves in the midst of a regiment of Gurkhas. It was the inevitable Army again. It seems that the Second Division of the Northern Army camped north of Delhi last night, and was now marching past the city to the Tomb of Safdar Jang. On Tuesday active operations are to be resumed, and there are rumours of an impending battle. This time the Northern Army is to remain on the defensive, and the Southern Army is to do the attacking; but I hear that the First Division of the Northern Army has been transferred to the Southern force in consequence. When you first see a Gurkha regiment, you think that a bit of the Japanese Army must have strayed into India by mistake. The men look the splendid fighting material they are, and you can well imagine that they climb like cats on a mountain side. You are struck, too, by their really merry demeanour, which contrasts strangely with the gravity of the Sikh and the Rajput. "Jolly little chaps! I remember the times I had with 'em in Burma," murmurs your companion; and jolly little chaps they are. Nowadays the Gurkha on service wears a slouch hat looped up at one side, veldt fashion, and they have given him khaki "boating shorts" which leave the knee bare. I saw one man in the old-fashioned dress of the Gurkha with the pork-pie forage cap; the new uniform looks a great improvement. A British soldier, who had apparently got separated from his battalion, wandered past us. A Gurkha slipped out of the ranks, thrust an orange into his hand,

and grinned with huge delight. Tommy produced another piece of fruit, pressed it on the Gurkha in exchange, and both shook hands as though they were blood brothers. Then the Gurkha, smiling and happy, trotted after his comrades. It was quite a pleasant incident.

How we got mixed up with the Second Division, how we were shrouded, as usual, in clouds of dust, how we bumped over bye-paths and dodged obstinate mountain battery mules, need not be related. The point is that at length we got clear, and found ourselves driving along the Gurgaon Road. A mile away, on the direct road to the Kutab Minar, dense volumes of dust marked the march of the Army. And when we turned homewards, a good three hours later, the column was still passing. A Division takes up a good deal of room, and when you have seen one once on an Indian road, a mile is about the best distance from which to contemplate it. The first camp you come to on the Gurgaon Road is the modest plot set apart for the Political Agents of the Bombay Presidency. The tents are arranged in two long rows, and at the end of them is a spacious drawing room tent, leading into another tent which will serve as a dining room. Just across the road is the camp of the Raj Kumars of the Presidency, who will be in charge of Mr. C. W. Waddington. Their dwellings are also unpretentious, as becomes young men; and they certainly have an example set them in the Spartan severity of Mr. Waddington's quarters.

Hard by is a special telegraph office, across a field or two a little hospital can be seen, and away in the distance—where the interminable Army is streaming along—are the lines set apart for the Aden Chiefs.

Let us follow this side of the road for a mile or two, before tackling the camps on the other side. The next is that of H. H. the Mir of Khairpur. If the Khairpur State is run with the smartness and energy shown at its Delhi camp, it must be a pattern to many native administrations. The Khairpur people were the first to start and the first to finish. Not even a bit of waste paper mars the general neatness. There is a trim archway over the entrance, and the paths are all carefully gravelled. Well-built open water-channels will keep the camp free from standing water if it rains in January, as everybody predicts. The Mir has a big reception tent, with *pukka* doors fitted with stained glass windows. In the centre of the plot is a huge raised dais of earth, upon which is an open *shamiana*. This is a camp which has been well and economically managed. The next camp, a little farther down the road, is that of H. H. the Maharajah of Idar, and as we enter it the gallant and soldierly Maharajah himself appears to greet us. Sir Pratap Singh looks as keen-eyed and as full of energy as ever he did. His activity is amazing. He is Honorary Colonel of the Imperial Cadet Corps, and had already put in a stiff morning parade with his young followers, near their camp, far away to the north of the city. Yet here he was, only an hour or two later, busily engaged in personally supervising the completion of his own camp. His Highness tells you that he feels it incumbent upon him to live with his Corps, and his camp will be chiefly used by his English guests, who include the Guards polo team. There will be many imposing figures in the procession at the State Entry into Delhi, but no more interesting personality than the Colonel of the Imperial Cadets, in his snow-white uniform.

Next is reached the camp of the Raja of Bansda, which will be used chiefly by his retainers; the Raja himself has taken a house in the adjacent village of Paharganj. Then comes the camp of the Chief of Miraj Senior, with a fine *shamiana* as its central feature. The Chief of Bhore was allotted a contiguous plot, but has elected to reside in a house in Delhi, near the Kabuli Gate. Finally, there is the spacious place set apart for the accommodation of the Bombay Durbaris. These gentlemen, however, have not taken kindly to the idea that they should live in camp. Plots are marked out for every one of them, but only about eight seemed to be occupied. The ground has been carefully prepared, and intersected by a network of paths. A big well has been sunk and water was reached while we were watching the operations.

The biggest Bombay Camps, however, are on the western side of the Gurgaon Road. H. H. the Maharajah of Kolhapur has here made very elaborate preparations. His camp has a large and not unpleasing garden, which contains, among other adjuncts, a couple of bandstands. His Highness has ordered a complete installation of the electric light. His tents and marquees occupy the centre of the camp, and the feudatory chiefs are grouped around him. He is bringing seven or eight hundred followers to Delhi. So, too, is H. H. the Rao of Cutch, whose camp is very carefully laid out. As one enters it, two great tents of a rich reddish-brown hue arrest the eye. These are both over a hundred years old, yet they look in an excellent state of preservation. They were woven and made in Cutch itself. Their interiors are of material of a handsome flowered pattern, the colours looking as fresh as though they were new. But the pride of the Cutch camp is the huge velvet *shamiana*. All its poles are of silver, the smaller ones solid. The Nawab of Junagadh also has a handsome reception tent in his camp; and his officials point with satisfaction to the great array of crotons decorating its approaches. The reception tent is reached through a double row of tents wherein will dwell the Amirs and the chief officials of the State. But the finest camp in the whole of the Bombay section is undoubtedly that of the Thakore Saheb of Bhavnagar, which was designed and constructed by the State Engineer, Mr. Proctor Sims. It is entered beneath a great archway, containing recesses wherein picturesque Arabs will sit and smoke. Rows of fine tents will accommodate the guests and the State officials. The central feature is a *shamiana* of noble proportions, lit by clusters of electric lamps. The Bhavnagar camp has been lavish in electrical illumination, but the arched entrance and the central drive are also furnished with powerful Kitson lights. Bhavnagar, too, has created a really successful garden, with dainty beds of flowers; but the most prominent landmark of the camp is the huge white flagstaff with its gilt top, and its properly squared yard, the best flagstaff in Delhi. The Rana of Porebunder has made a triumphal archway at his gates covered with striking pictures by native artists. His camp is well arranged, and the precaution of placing every tent on a firm raised plinth has been taken. There are far too few plinths to the multitude of tents at Delhi, as people will discover if the rain comes. The camp of the Thakore Saheb of Morvi presents no semblance either of arrangement or decoration; it is in a very backward state, and the less said about it the better. The Thakore Saheb of Limri has no very striking features in his camp, and neither has the Raja of Bariya. The Nawab of Janjira has constructed a small but trim camp lit by Kitson lights. H. H. the Sultan of Shehr and Makalla, H. H. the Thakore Saheb of Gondal, and the Thakore Saheb of Palitana, have all taken bungalows. On the whole, the camps of the Bombay chiefs make an excellent appearance. It may be convenient to mention that they are no longer in charge of Captain F. W. Wodehouse, I.S.C., who has become an attaché to the Foreign

Office; he handed them over on the 10th instant to Captain J. G. Carter, I.S.C., of the Bombay Political Department.

The residence of one more of the Bombay rulers must not escape mention. The Nawab of Cambay has sought a quiet retreat in the very heart of Delhi. It is in the narrow, noisy, crowded thoroughfare known as Sirkiwalla Bazaar. You turn suddenly from the bazaar down a close grimy alley with lofty walls, scarcely wider than your carriage, and emerge into a broad courtyard. A few steps through a battered archway and you are in an old garden, a veritable "haunt of ancient peace." At the far end is the wide entrance to a house. You are in a place with a history. This quiet garden, and the old mansion, formed the residence of the Wazirs of the Emperors of Delhi. Look at the carved and painted ceilings in the reception rooms; they are worth the trouble, although the light is dim. Here is a refuge from the chilly nights and the glare of noontide. Not a sound from the roaring city without penetrates this cloistered seclusion. It is a little mouldering; the rooms have a faint odour of age; the garden terraces are moss-grown; a hint of mildewed neglect pervades the place. But once you are within its shelter, the dust and the clatter and the bustle distract you no more.

V.

IN MARBLE HALLS.

December 16.

THERE is one place in Delhi, the first sight of which is surely unforgettable. It is enshrined behind the Titanic rose-pink walls of the vast Fort, those huge masses that look as though they were built for all time. You would never dream that such grim portals could conceal a retreat so enchanting. The great battlements tower above you as you enter a formidable gateway, and stand wondering in the centre of a gigantic hall with vaulted roof. It is like the nave of a cathedral. Beyond it, you enter an open space that is called a courtyard, but is the size of a London square. You cross it, advance through another mighty archway and confront the Diwan-i-Am, or Hall of Public Audience. It is hard to realise what is the normal appearance of the Diwan-i-Am, for it has been transformed to serve as the scene of the State Investiture, and afterwards of the State Ball, next month. In other times, you gather, it is an arcade with red stone pillars and engrailed arches, walled on the farthest side only. Now as you approach it the eye only perceives smooth brick-red walls, giving no earnest of splendour within.

Nor does the interior impress you at first. How can it?

> Scaffolding veils the walls,
> And dim dust floats and falls.

The pillars near you, you discover, are of iron and wood covered with painted plaster. The hall of Aurangzeb has been doubled in size, that Britons may dance therein. For the present it is given over to the carpenter and the plasterer. You are about to pass by it, when through the vista of arches you catch the pale gleam of marble. You draw nearer, stumbling amid planks and ropes, and stand before the high marble recess, with pillars and canopy, whereon once was reared the Peacock Throne. The walls are inlaid with pictures of birds and foliage, done in precious stones. What untold wealth the hordes of conquering invaders must have torn from them! Where jewels once sparkled, only the cavities that held them remain. Yet vandal hands have failed to destroy the noble majesty of the recess itself, and you can whip your imagination into picturing it as Bernier saw it. Here on high sat the Emperor, clad in gold-embroidered white satin, his turban glittering with diamonds, his neck ringed with pearls. Here he gazed upon his nobles and ministers, upon pillars hung with brocades, floors strewn with silken carpets, canopies veiling the arched roof. And here, amid a medley of the real and the sham, which it needs an effort to acquiesce in, the great gathering in honour of the first Emperor of all India is to hold its revels.

You pass from the clangour of hammer and chisel into the courtyard beyond, and are at last face to face with the loveliest retreat in this ruined fairyland. It is the Diwan-i-Khas, or Hall of Private Audience, a pavilion of pure white marble with an open portico, and domes on slender pillars at the four corners. Let us get over the rather jarring alterations now being made. In this Hall the guests at the State Ball will sit down to supper, which is scarcely congruous. However, save in the single matter of the architectural blending of the real and the shoddy, any sentimental regrets about the uses to which these two Halls are to be put would be ridiculous. No hallowed memories cluster around the Diwan-i-Khas. No historic traditions will be outraged by its use as a supper room. Shah Jehan and his successors used it for audiences, and within its reticent shelter they dallied with their women; that is all. For Englishmen, its chief associations are that within it the late Queen's health was proposed when the Palace was captured in 1857, and that on a famous Sunday it was used for the Thanksgiving Service when Delhi fell. It is flanked on one side by the Emperor's Private Apartments, and on the other by the Royal Baths. These have been temporarily united with the main building by structures in keeping with the general design, constructed of inexpensive materials. To read about, they may convey an idea of atrocious bad taste; but I can only say that when you have overcome the first repellant feeling which ensues when you realise that the buildings are not all real, you are constrained to admit that the imitations are amazingly clever. And after the æsthetic sense has been lulled, you pass with small reluctance to a state of approval, for you recognise that not one stone of the original structures has been injured, and that when the Durbar is a thing of the past, they will rapidly regain their original form. Perhaps it is not necessary to indicate in detail the changes that have been made. Hot-water pipes and the electric light, however agreeable and illuminating, are best forgotten in Shah Jehan's abode of bliss.

It stands in the farthest confines of the spacious grounds enclosed by the Fort, on the very verge of the east wall. From it you may look out towards the rising sun, across the bed of the Jumna, now dry and covered with undergrowth, save where there is a glint of water far away. But you have no eyes for the distant prospect. You stand entranced at the marvel within. The sumptuous simplicity and purity of the whole interior hold you spellbound. It is a dream in marble, an enchanting spectacle of pillars and arches decorated with gold and inlay work, of delicate pierced tracery, of cool vistas of shining white, blended with adornments in the softest hues. And yet there is no excess of gorgeousness in it, nothing to dazzle, no trace of unduly rich colouring; the dominant note is always the white marble. The Sleeping Apartments convey the same effect, and there projects from the wall a small room and balcony, screened at the outer edge by marble lattice-work, where you fain would linger for hours. The proportions of the central pavilion are so perfect, the conception of its creator so satisfying, that only by degrees do you realise how much of the first fine splendour has vanished. The innumerable jewels have been gouged from the pillars and panels ; the ceiling is no longer appropriate; of the throne, nothing but the marble platform remains; in the baths, some nameless destroyer has whitewashed the upper walls.

Yet you can conceive what it must have been like when Shah Jehan was still supreme, and the dark shadow of that ultimate dungeon at Agra had not closed round him for ever. Then the jewelled walls of the zenana glittered in the morning light, save in the tiny room where even now a vague apprehension of violated privacy overtakes the prying stranger. In the central hall, where in later years the blazing glories of the Peacock Throne were enshrined, the supporting piers were flashing with precious stones. The ceiling was of solid plates of burnished silver. The golden inlay work was still fresh from the artist's hands. The light streamed in through marble lattices and stained glass, or was filtered through luminous alabaster. The very baths were richly inlaid and jewelled. In one, dozens of little fountains spurted rosewater, wherein the royal ladies dipped their jewels on rising. In others, cunning devices enabled the voluptuous monarch to bathe at will without menial aid. Underground passages permitted the royal favourites to wander from the Zenana to the baths unseen by curious eyes. Close at hand was the Private Mosque, its pure marble arches—still saved intact from sacrilegious hands—chastely carved and moulded. And through all these exquisite structures the cool refreshing glimmer of the marble. For you must think of these joyous retreats, not as they look beneath this hard blue sky, in the keen winter air, but as they were when the shadows were swiftly lengthening at the close of a day of fierce heat. Without were lovely gardens, screened from the vulgar gaze, with plashing fountains and tiny cascades. And you may picture Shah Jehan seated in a wide pavilion amid the trees, where lamps shone even amid the tumbling waterfalls, and the night air was laden with the scent of flowers, and beneath the tropic moon the Hall of Audience took unto itself a pale unearthly beauty. No longer then will the words the Emperor inscribed upon the panels of the Diwan-i-Khas sound commonplace by familiarity. For he spoke the simple truth when he wrote: "If a Paradise be on the face of the earth, it is this, it is this, it is this!"

One aspect more of this, the very heart and centre of the Mogul Empire, remains to be told, though it strikes an abrupt contrast. Through the dainty lattices, a glimpse of the distant river, spanned by a huge iron bridge, more solid and enduring than the walls of Delhi. Where once were leafy bowers, the blunt square outlines of British barracks. And at the entrance to the marble halls, quiet, alert, reliant, with ruddy English face, a young soldier of the Gunners.

VI.

FROM A HILL TOP.

December 17.

IT was really a ridge that bisects the Grand Trunk Road a good seventeen miles south of the Imperial City, and it had taken several weary hours to get there by a circuitous route around the flanks of both Armies. This was the position. Delhi had been captured by the invaders, and the Government had fled to the town of Gurgaon, twenty miles or so to the south-west. A weakened Division of the triumphant foe was entrenched six miles south of Delhi. The imaginary main army of the invaders was far away at Meerut. The Southern Army had been reinforced by a whole Infantry Division, a Cavalry Brigade, and a 30-pounder battery. They were now about to endeavour to push back the weakened enemy, and cut them off from the fords and bridges across the Jumna that led to Meerut. On this day they were four or five miles north of Gurgaon, and were in contact with their adversaries. Sitting at noontide on the crest of the ridge, the whole scene of the operations lay outspread in one vast panorama. It was, for once, a perfectly clear and almost windless day. To the south, the rich fertile well-wooded plain seemed to stretch out for an illimitable distance. To the north, the ridge sloped gently into a broad shallow valley, which in its turn rose a mile or two away into another low ridge crowned with woods. Beyond, Delhi-wards, were the tall slender outlines of the Kutab Minar, and behind it there floated in mid-air, seemingly ethereal and unsubstantial, a pale silvery-white dome. The depression before us extended right and left for miles, and was the main position of the Southern Army. Some one who knows something of active service said that you might go through a whole campaign without getting such a perfect view of a large force actually at work.

As a spectacle it was rather disappointing. The field was so large that it impressed by reason of its spaciousness, but by little else. You gained some notion of the elbow-room an army requires for its task nowadays, but the actual movements were represented by little brown masses where infantry were marching, by clouds of dust that marked the passage of cavalry, and by smoke where some batteries were firing with black powder. Other batteries were unseen, even from the ridge in rear, and their position could only be guessed by the movements of the gallopers who raced about the valley at breakneck speed. As for the enemy, they were from first to last discreetly invisible. We saw nothing of them, the reason being, as we afterwards found, that they had received information at noon that their communications with Umballa had been cut, and were therefore about to retire on the Jumna to join their friends at Meerut. The actual operations may be left to military correspondents to describe. These are only a few impressions of a casual spectator. But we gathered, and indeed it seemed obvious, that the movements were preliminary to a general advance in full force the next day. If the enemy could be tempted out of their position, so much the better. But, as events showed, they had determined to withdraw.

In a rugged hollow immediately below us were some ammunition carts belonging to a horse battery, with a few gunners in attendance. Though within our view, they were perfectly concealed. On the rising slope on the farther side of the valley was a long, narrow, dark mass of men and horses. The glass showed them to be a cavalry brigade, dismounted and evidently awaiting orders. Groups of horsemen hovered in front of them and on their right. On the edge of the Grand Trunk Road a horse battery was throwing shells over the ridge. Still farther away, a heavy battery was pounding; the boom of its guns filled the air, but it was not visible to the remote observers. The eye ranged on to the point where one knew the main body of the Southern Infantry had entrenched themselves; but there was much jungle and undergrowth about, and even powerful field-glasses failed to reveal their exact position. Yet farther, a captive balloon floated aloft, indicating that somewhere in its neighbourhood was the head-quarters of the Army. There was no mistaking the principal camp. The gaze lit upon it behind a stretch of woods—a medley of baggage carts and animals, with here and there a stray tent. It must have been impossible for the enemy to discern it, even from the topmost platform of the Kutab Minar. On the horizon on the extreme right could be traced the line of the Jumna. There seemed to be heavy fighting going on there, but its nature was not ascertainable. Add to the picture stray horsemen galloping madly, lines of carts wandering aimlessly about the Grand Trunk Road, the occasional whirl of a squadron of cavalry scurrying on some unexplained errand; remember that the sound of firing and the frequent thunder of heavy guns were borne upwards to our hill-top; and you have a fairly complete idea of one phase of modern war operations, as they present themselves to the onlooker. All that was lacking of the stern reality of actual warfare was the long drone of the soaring shell, the whistling of the bullets—and the dead and wounded.

To the untrained eye it looked rather a jumble, as probably most military undertakings appear to all save the directing brain; and yet, after prolonged contemplation of the scene, certain main features could be followed. It was clear, for instance, that some sort of turning movement of cavalry on the flank immediately before you was either meditated or in progress. Plainly the guns in the centre of the valley were shelling the enemy's main position at long range. The sounds of conflict, far away to the right on the edge of the Jumna, were understandable even to the layman. The right flank of the Army was pushing northwards along the river bank, to seize the bridges across the canal and the river. If they could accomplish that, the morrow might be theirs. They would have enveloped the Northern Army in a sort of horse-shoe formation, and cut off their communication with the imaginary main Army at Meerut. If the attack was pressed home, the invaders would be crowded back towards the river, with nothing but a narrow line of retreat through Delhi left open to them. But it was only gradually that this became clear, and meanwhile one was mainly conscious of the seeming confusion. The fighting line is the only place for excitement. To look upon these little brown dots, and clouds of dust and smoke, spread out at your feet over the whole country-side, only conveyed a curious sense of detachment to the onlooker in his eyrie. I write as a mere civilian. The trained soldier may have found the spectacle engrossing enough ; but with no visible enemy, and no means of knowing how the movements were progressing, there seemed nothing very stirring about it.

Presently there came a diversion. A messenger or two had cantered along the valley and vanished over the ridge right before us. Not long afterwards a swarm of cavalry came thundering back over the brow. It looked as though the attempt to turn the left flank was being temporarily abandoned.

The Brigade in reserve behind the ridge sprang to their horses. In two minutes the whole force was streaming headlong along the valley towards the right flank. At least that was the presumption; but from the moment the movement commenced, not a man could be seen. All that was visible was one long dense cloud of dust. A passer-by offered a surmise. It looked, he said, as though the enemy were pressing the right flank, which had pushed rather far ahead. If that was the case, there was little chance that the Southern Army would get much nearer Delhi that day. Next morning a battle would be almost inevitable.

We retraced our steps as the sun began to sink. Five miles away, we came to a peaceful village. Big substantial houses, each in its compound, stood around a broad green sward shaded by ancient trees. Upon the turf outside the village school, smiling children sat chanting their lesson to a venerable schoolmaster. Close by some mahouts were scrubbing two or three elephants. A row of placid villagers sat on a wall and watched the process with intense interest. Women passed on their way to the well. The air was still, and the little scene quiet and peaceful. A native official who spoke good English—one of the legion of judicial subordinates—strolled up. We paused to talk with him. He knew nothing of the rival Armies, and had no notion that fighting was in progress near him. And yet, even as he spoke, the sound of big guns smote his incurious ear.

VII.

IN BATTLE ARRAY.

December 18.

IN official despatches, I believe, it is described as a "general action." It is not my purpose to discuss its military significance, for I am not a war correspondent, or even a soldier. I can only put down what I saw, and how it struck a layman.

We arrived this morn at the great Mausoleum of Safdar Jang, some miles south of Delhi, on the road to the Kutab Minar. Forthwith we were in the midst of alarums and excursions. This time, be it understood, we were with the Northern Army, which was acting more or less on the defensive. On the previous day we had been well behind the Southern Army. We climbed to the roof of the massive gateway leading to the Tomb. The country to the south was thickly wooded, but immediately to the west was a broad dusty plain, a mile or two wide, flanked by ridges. Due east, a shady road led to the Tomb of the Emperor Humayun, a couple of miles away. But it was hard to discern the operations southward ; the trees were too thick.

We were, it seemed, on the right flank of the Northern Army ; and it did not take ten minutes' inspection of the scene from that convenient roof to discover that the right flank was not faring well. There were villages scattered among the ridges to the west; the glass revealed bits of houses here and there among the trees; faint sounds of firing drifted from their neighbourhood. Presently, across the dusty plain that has been mentioned, came batches of infantry in retreat. The enemy were clearing the villages. Evidently the right flank was being driven in.

But this was only the outskirts of the fight that was plainly developing. The evidence of one's ears suggested that it was not on the flanks, but in the centre of the position, that the hardest fighting was taking place. From Humayun's Tomb the smoke of a heavy battery arose. We deserted our gateway, and drove thither, in the hope that the situation would become clearer. The approach to the Tomb is a mass of ruins. You are amid the crumbling remains of an older Delhi, a veritable mournful desolation. Figure them with baggage camels and mules, casual groups of infantry, hurrying staff officers, and all the paraphernalia of an army, grouped about among the decaying walls, and you may get some idea of the strange contrasts that presented themselves. Behind a roofless house, tucked in amid the hollows, were a row of squat, dumpy howitzers with their muzzles gaping skywards. Beside each sat a group of gunners, manifestly weary, apparently mightily bored. Perched on an adjacent remnant of a once lofty building was a knot of men taking observations. At a signal from them, the team manning one howitzer sprang into activity. There was a flash and a roar, and before the smoke had cleared, the howitzer was being made ready again. Leaving the battery steadily pounding away, we clambered up to the roof of Humayun's Tomb, where was quite a little throng of umpires and transport officers. It commanded a wide expanse of country; and yet—I write it to show how little one can perceive of a modern battle unless actually engaged in it—we could see practically nothing. Remember that at this time over forty thousand men were more or less in action along a semi-circular front of at least ten miles. Remember that we were on the top of a mighty tomb which overlooked an immense area, and was dangerously within range of the guns of the foe. Yet of the operations, all that remained visible were the howitzers roaring away below us, some cavalry and mounted infantry wandering along the road we had traversed, suspicious clouds of dust beyond the Tomb of Safdar Jang, and a few shreds of the transport huddled together in one or two clearings. It is true that the thick woods were a disadvantage to the onlooker. I set down only what came under my own notice. This is simply an attempt to explain how the warfare of to-day fails to satisfy the demands of the ignorant spectator. The best advice that can be given to the ingenuous layman is to stick to Drury Lane. The late Augustus Harris understood the spectacular side of war far better than our ablest Generals.

My companion suggested that as there were no bullets about, we might as well get into the firing line. I assented with heroic alacrity. And here I must explain that the fords across the Jumna were the most vital points in the defences of the Northern Army. Therefore it was their left flank, and not their right flank, where we commenced to watch the action, which was the crucial position. But, as a matter of fact, it was against their centre, and not against either flank, that the General commanding the Southern Army delivered the attack we were about to witness at close quarters. If General Wodehouse could break the Northern centre, he would have split the enemy's forces. This he gallantly attempted to perform.

We went south for a couple of miles along a road lined with trees. Guns roared behind us and far ahead of us, and on our right broke forth the crackle of rifles. But the road was absolutely deserted. The heart of the battle was still to seek. Presently we arrived at a gap in the trees. The firing was nearer now. Three or four native troopers came into view on a contiguous hillock. We stumbled through a little ravine and clambered up beside them. At last we could see things! Before us and on our left and right was a stretch of open country, partly patches of cultivation, partly mere wilderness. Beyond it a long high ridge crowned at intervals by ruins. Across the centre of this open tract, not a mile away, a line of little figures was hastening in the direction of Humayun's Tomb.

Field hospital sections, camp followers, ammunition mules, divers details, all were in eager retreat from the ridge. It did not take us long to reach and pass through them, and next moment we were in the firing line. Two battalions—one British, the other native—were steadily retiring at this point in extended order, and as far as the gaze wandered to the left, similar movements were in progress. The Northerners' centre was being driven in; they had forsaken the ridge, and were withdrawing upon the Mausoleum. And even as we halted, the sky-line became suddenly alive. Tiny doll-like forms were running over the ridge, dropping for a moment, firing, and hurrying forward again. The enemy were in sight.

In less time than it takes to tell, the whole country-side was covered with troops. Infantry poured across the ridge, swarming everywhere like locusts, and keeping up a steady fusillade at the regiments in retreat. It was just as though they had sprung up out of the ground. The Northerners quickened their retirement, and their firing grew feebler as the intensity of the attack increased. I write without knowledge, but there seemed to be little serious attempt to take cover. At the edge of a spinney, I came upon two detachments of native infantry, standing up and blazing away at one another at a range of a hundred yards; but there happened to be no British officer near them. Then a battery topped the ridge, and began to play upon the retreating troops. It was time for us to withdraw also, and we turned and plodded through heavy fields to the road. This done, it was a fine sight to watch the clouds of Southerners advancing on a front visible for two or three miles. It was a regular infantry duel. How far it would have been possible on active service I cannot say ; but the ground looked broken enough to permit of a far more prolonged defence than was attempted. The battery on the ridge was still plugging away ; other batteries were coming into action on the left. A regiment of Gurkhas came tramping along the road, followed by another of stalwart Sikhs ; both had abandoned the attempt to check the advance, and were concentrating at the Tomb. Just then a horse battery tore up from the rear. You would have thought that nothing could stop the impetuous rush of the horses ; but in an instant they had swerved into a roadside hollow, and were covering the retreat by answering the battery on the ridge.

A knot of horsemen approached, followed by a native trooper bearing a little Union Jack. Lord Kitchener and his staff were riding along the firing line. They dismounted on the hillock where we stood. The Commander-in-Chief, a little in advance of the rest, surveyed the progress of the fight through his glass. Some incident attracted his attention, and he pointed it out to the others. As he stood there, with arm outstretched, he looked a curiously familiar figure. You somehow felt that you had seen that tall khaki-clad form, that face with the steady, searching eyes, those keen glances along the line of battle, in just that attitude, wearing just that expression, dozens of times before. There is really no need for anybody to go and see anything nowadays. The illustrated papers do their work so well that they deprive the most striking scene of any sense of novelty.

To describe the remainder of the action would perhaps be wearisome. The story must be compressed. Seeing that the centre had been driven back, we returned eventually to our morning's coign of vantage at the Tomb of Safdar Jang. We had left the Northerners' right flank there. Now it had disappeared into the wooded country nearer Delhi, and over the open plain were advancing guns and regiments; far away towards the Kutab, in a confused mass, the baggage train of the triumphant assailants. Yet the Northerners were not far away; there was still rifle fire from the woods, and it needed attention. And here was witnessed the strangest incident of the day. Knots of villagers hung nervously about the road before the Tomb. A tight-rope walker, scantily clad, appeared among them, followed by two or three men with poles, and another with a tom-tom. The poles were put up at the roadside, the rope stretched, and the sad-eyed performer commenced his pitiful feats. The villagers clustered round in a moment. Not a hundred yards away, two companies of the Argyll and Sutherland Highlanders were advancing in skirmishing order against the waspish snipers among the trees. A dashing horse battery was whirling up in support, clearing embankments, ditches, boulders, furrowed fields, in one wild resistless rush. Beyond, regiment after regiment of the Southern Army were closing in and entrenching themselves upon the hard-won position. Highlanders in action, and horse batteries at a gallop over rough country, sights that many home-staying Englishmen would give their ears to see, and all within a radius of three hundred yards! And yet the mild Hindoo placidly turns his back and prefers the tight-rope.

As the sun began to sink, significant clouds of dust on the extreme left, a good two miles away, revealed the point where the Southerners were attempting a wide sweeping movement of cavalry in flank in the direction of Delhi. How a cavalry brigade immediately beneath us trotted off in support, how the Northerners' guns spake warning from unsuspected recesses in the woods, how the flanking movement dwindled into a meaningless reconnaissance, and how jaded cavalry and tired Highlanders alike came back to the shelter of Safdar Jang, time does not suffice to tell. Camp fires were beginning to flicker on the plain as twilight fell upon the scene. The Southerners had made good their advance, and had hemmed in the foe on the banks of the Jumna. Nothing was left for the Northerners but a hasty retreat across the river. And as we drove off through the dust and darkness, the sound of guns contesting the approaches to the ford and bridge mercilessly shattered the stillness of night.

VIII.

THE CANVAS CITY.

December 23.

YOU people away in the radiant South perhaps picture us engrossed in the preparations for the Durbar, talking of nothing but elephants and armies and the Great Ones of the Land. If you do, you are wrong. The Durbar is only a mere incident which has brought us all together, a fortuitous collection of chilly atoms of humanity, in the middle of a dusty plain ; but what actually absorbs our attention is the problem of warming our canvas abodes when the cold sweeps in with a rush at sunset. If you are a real bigwig—and every other man you meet here is a bigwig of sorts—you have a large double-pole tent with a fire-place made of white-washed mud. It is sometimes an advantage not to be a bigwig, and in the matter of fire-places there are certainly points in favour of decent obscurity. The square chimney outside the larger tents gives an earnest of cosiness within, which is not always realised in the event. You modestly approach the dwelling of greatness, and as you peer within the portals you discern the physical embodiment of such limited fame as India can confer, looming, impressive but only vaguely defined, in the midst of dense clouds of acrid smoke.

The fire-places have other defects. Sometimes the crackling wood projects sparks into the middle of the tent; and the average time that it takes to wipe out a tent when fairly aflame is four minutes. The spark difficulty, however, can be overcome by wire guards, and so far I have only heard of three tents suffering destruction. But a new pattern of lamp stove, with which the smaller tents are equipped, is infinitely preferable. It is not the people in the big marquees, but those in the trim little Swiss Cottage tents, who are most comfortably off when the temperature falls. If you treat the lamp stove tenderly, it gives you reasonable warmth. If you don't—most people don't—it diffuses an odour of kerosene until your tent suggests the business premises of an Italian warehouseman.

But you will be lucky if you do not live in an atmosphere of kerosene in any case; for there are the white ants to be reckoned with also. You awake in the morning to be greeted with the pleasing intelligence that an army of these pertinacious insects has eaten through a cabin trunk, and has just concluded a banquet upon your only frock-coat. Then there is a hasty lifting of dhurries and matting, and kerosene is recklessly poured upon the layer of grey sand from the Jumna upon which every tent has been erected. There seems to be a legend in Delhi that fine sand from the Jumna is to the white ant anathema, and that it will not take up its abode where the sand is strewn. Hear now the conclusion of the whole matter from a deeply-interested investigator: there is nothing the white ant seems to doat upon more than sand from the Jumna, unless it be frock-coats. The saving grace about this ubiquitous pest is his aversion to kerosene.

But despite the little discomforts inseparable from camp life in a somewhat rigorous climate, this period of sojourn in the Canvas City is very pleasant You are roused and crawl shivering from beneath a mountain of blankets and rezais. A cup of scalding hot tea encourages you to face the keen air without, and you sally forth just as the sun is shouldering itself above the Ridge. Many people elect to take their morning exercise upon horseback, but there are a very large number of bicycles in camp. The horse is rather an unknown quantity in this extraordinary assemblage. If he will face a steam lorry, he may shy at an elephant; when you have induced him to confront an elephant without quailing, the amazing sight of a red coach drawn by four camels may send him flying headlong into the tents sacred to a Lieutenant-Governor. On the other hand, the roads have greatly improved during the last few days, and bicycling is no longer entirely toilsome. In a gentle ride along the Alipur Road, which traverses the centre of the camp, you may chance to meet half the celebrities of India. One wonders what the wide-eyed stranger from England thinks of this wonderful thoroughfare, and of the scene witnessed there in the early morning. On either side are the interminable tents, stretching away for miles.

Yet it is not the tents that fix your attention, but the motley throng on the road. You meet first, perhaps, a long string of fifty or a hundred horses belonging to a Native State, out for their daily exercise, shying violently as the little engine of the Camp Railway goes puffing by, and becoming absolutely unmanageable when the band of a crack cavalry regiment, practising casually by the roadside, suddenly bursts forth into a popular air. Then a detachment of British infantry, stolid but cheerful, trudges across your path. Follows a train of excitable baggage mules, returning belated from the manœuvres. Then a row of shambling camels, carrying supplies to an outlying camp. Not description, but a simple catalogue, is needed to convey an idea of the spectacle. Gaudy carriages containing native chiefs, with escorts of wild lancers; a batch of Beluchi notables, tittuping along, looking the reckless caterans they are; English girls with a rosy colour that you only see in Bombay on mail days in the cold weather; Bengali babus, with heads swathed for the nonce in weird puggarees, and teeth chattering; men whose names have been familiar in India for a quarter of a century, and who have grown grey in her service; a knot of weird mountaineers from Sikkim, with hats like inverted flower pots, crowned with peacock's feathers; a file of retinue elephants, their foreheads daubed with crude colours, lumbering heavily past; whining beggars, ash-smeared devotees, creaking bullock-carts, brightly-clad postmen, soldier orderlies on bicycles, globe-trotters on motor-cars, alert mounted policemen, Tommies in khaki, frowsy coolies, officers driving neat dog-carts; the Commander-in-Chief, taking his morning ride; the knightly figure of Sir Pratap Singh, in the smart khaki and light blue undress uniform of the Imperial Cadet Corps, astride a fine horse; the Viceregal teams, putting in a final trial spin before the representative of the King-Emperor arrives: really, it would take a whole article just to chronicle the sights to be seen on the Alipur Road in a run before breakfast.

You return from your ride with your cheeks aglow, and your blood at last warm in your veins. The sun is by this time high enough to have modified the temperature of your dressing tent, and you tub in comparative comfort. The curious thing about the Delhi climate is that in the mid-day hours the thermometer climbs to quite a respectable point. You have to adjust your clothing to the welcome change, and flannel suits or thin tweeds are for a brief space not an impossibility. By the time high noon has arrived, you have forgotten the freezing misery of early morning, and when you sit down to tiffin, you are even inclined to fancy that the spacious mess tent is a little stuffy. But the delusion does not long cloud your mind, and when the time approaches for your evening drive, you are clamouring once more for your thickest suit, and an ulster, and the heaviest rug you can find. A pale mist is rising as you prepare to start, and you are conscious that the friendly sun is disappearing for the night.

Most of the tent-dwellers turn towards the Imperial City when they set out again at eventide. In the morning, a ride through the camp; in the evening, a drive into Delhi. That is the accepted programme; I do not know why it should be so, except that there is a glamour about the city in the twilight, which it unquestionably fails to reveal in the pitiless morning. You may go, if you will, to a point where the rose-red walls of the Fort are flushed in the glow of the setting sun. Or you may slowly traverse the Chandni Chauk, that marvellous artery of Delhi which epitomises the magic and the mystery of an Eastern city. I have not seen any spot which so nearly approximates to the accepted ideas of the Oriental bazaar, as does the Chandni Chauk just now. To begin with, it is a mass of traffic. Picture the roaring stream that converges upon the Mansion House, multiply it three times over, change the hansoms into bullock-carts, and the four-wheelers into clumsy ekkas, throw in some stray camels and elephants, mix with a seething throng of native humanity and you may get a faint notion of the Chandni Chauk at sunset. But for the solid granite buildings familiar to every Londoner, you must substitute the shabby shops, each holding a king's ransom, where the obsequious jewellers of Delhi display their wares. You must imagine the narrow counters, gorgeous with silks and brocades and heavy embroideries, so tempting and so costly. You must fill in the pavements blocked by the sellers of fruit, with piles of juicy and refreshing produce. You must figure the broad avenue, with its umbrageous trees which the City of London can never hope to see. You must add the glaring lights, the masses of colour, the noise and the hubbub, the raucous conversations in stentorian tones which Cheapside knoweth not. And finally, you must conceive those mysterious upper storeys, with their wooden balconies, their reticent lattices, their dim alluring mysteries, where are glimpses of vague figures with gleaming armlets and shining necklaces, telling of an unwritten aspect of many-sided Delhi. Truly the Chandni Chauk at sunset is an amazing place.

You snuggle down amid your rugs as you turn finally towards home and dinner; and you are thankful for your humble stove when the moment arrives for you to change once more. There is no superfluous formality about a Durbar Camp in its preliminary stages. This is not a climate for unnecessary niceties of costume. To-night I saw four eminent civilians, one soldier not unknown to fame, and a famous war artist who has been through at least fifteen campaigns, dining in their overcoats, and openly shuddering with intense chilliness at that. Somehow the cold seems to trouble the newly arrived Englishman even more than the thin-blooded Anglo-Indian who has endured the tropics for years. It searches into every nook and cranny, and takes unresisting possession of the

Canvas City. There is no escaping it. Neither stoves nor mud fire-places enable you to evade it. The electric lamps amid the long lines of tents only serve to accentuate the misty wintry outlook. I scrawl this at a late hour with fingers that can scarcely hold the pen. There is only one inviting spot, and that is bed, with a multiplicity of blankets.

IX.

INDIA'S BAZAAR.

December 26.

AWAY towards the Delhi end of the Alipur Road, not far from the yellow flags which mark the Nizam's Camp, there arises amidst the trees a huge white building with a tastefully decorated front. This is the great Art Exhibition, initiated by Lord Curzon in order that the Durbar visitors may realise the importance of the arts and crafts of India, and in the hope of reviving ancient industries now fast dying out. When I had the privilege of a "private view" to-day, an army of workmen was getting everything in readiness for the opening ceremony, fixed for Tuesday, December 30th. But almost all the exhibits were in position, and it was possible to gain a very good idea of the scene, as it will be viewed by the Viceroy's guests. To give within the scope of a short article a detailed description of the collection would be impossible. In journeys extending over several months, Dr. George Watt and Mr. Percy Brown have ransacked India, from Peshawar to far off Mandalay, and from Nepal to Travancore. Within one building there is displayed all that is best in the gold and silver work, the embroidery, the carving, the metal, stone, glass and earthen ware, the carpet making, the weaving, and the innumerable minor crafts which give employment to thousands of skilled Indian workmen.

Standing amidst the art ware of a vast country, noted for centuries for its craftsmen, one realises the almost insurmountable difficulties the arrangement of the collection involved. The very nature of the scheme made complete success impossible. On the one hand there was to be a representation of the highest forms of Indian art; on the other hand there was planned a display of such a character as would attract many purchasers, and thus financially benefit the craftsmen whose work was shown. The two main objects were in a sense contradictory. To view, under the best conditions, the highest Indian art, one needs a small collection of superlative excellence, a collection in which every article can be examined with the greatest care, and in which no crowding or approach to duplication distract the attention. But without a large selection, and without the inclusion of designs displaying but little difference, the financial success of the scheme would be jeopardised. Something had to be sacrificed. Dr. Watt has sacrificed the artistic; and in this way.

The first impression of the visitor is this. A large hall, the walls of which are hung with carpets, filled with stalls and counters laden with an immense miscellaneous assortment of goods. In one place is a silver department, in another piles of cloths and mats and brocades; here a mass of brass work, there a display of carved or inlaid articles. It is a vast bazaar ; a huge departmental store. One expected an attendant to say : "The jewellery department is upstairs." But here again one of two courses had to be taken. The various art works could be placed in their proper setting, or divided in a way which would make comparison easy. One room might have been devoted to Burmese work alone, another to the Punjab, a third to Bombay or Sind. A scheme by which the *kincobs* of Ahmedabad and the brocades of Surat were displayed in a room lined by Gujarat carving and filled solely by Gujarat work would have been the more artistic. But the practical side of the exhibition could not be neglected, and the grouping has been made according to the nature of exhibits. Thus in one stand the silver work of Cutch is contrasted with that of Burma and Benares ; in another the visitor can compare the embroidery of Kashmir with that of Gujarat, the Punjab and Madras ; at a third the inlaid work of Bombay lies side by side with specimens from Surat. It is a plan which will encourage purchases. The visitor who wants brass work will not have to search a dozen rooms, the seeker after brocades will find at one spot all the best that India can produce. Thus owing to the quantity of the exhibits and the method of grouping, the Art Exhibition, with its waving banners near the roof, is more like a big shop than anything else.

This is, however, but the criticism of a first impression. When one closely inspects the actual work displayed, one forgets the general appearance of the building. The Exhibition is not a place in which to spend a single hour. To appreciate all its beauties and the wonderful variety in its rooms a long day would hardly suffice. Every foot contains gems of Indian handiwork. The walls, which at a first cursory glance seem to have no special feature, are found to exhibit some beautiful carving. Here is a Bhavnagar house with a balcony, designed by Mr. Proctor Sims, the State Engineer; there a frontage of Agra stone work; next a massive and curiously carved door from Mysore; then a model house from Nepal; further on others from Madras and Lahore. Some contain interiors fitted up in a style characteristic of the part from which they come; all are magnificent specimens of skilful craftsmanship. But what can one say of the exhibits? The first class alone—metal wares and ornaments—contains gold and silver wares, enamelled and Niello wares, damascened and encrusted wares, copper and brass wares, and tinned, painted and lacquered wares. And the specimens come from every part of India and Burma. And the exhibition contains ten classes sub-divided into fifty divisions, every division containing the curious, the beautiful, and the interesting. The gorgeous brocades and silks; the delicate laces in the selection of which Lady Curzon spent so much time; the carved ivory; the inlaying with mother-of-pearl ; the leather wares ; the varnished and wax work ; the pile carpets ; the expensive mats from Midnapur, Tinnevelly and Ganjam ; the pottery ; the gold and silver wire and braiding—these and many other lovely things are to be seen upon the tables, tempting the visitor to take back with him some specimen of Indian art. The first impression is one of bewilderment at the extent of the display ; the second a sense of shame at one's ignorance of the artistic wealth of Great Britain's greatest dependency.

An inspection of the central hall does not exhaust the treasures of India's bazaar. The loan collection is full of interesting and valuable things, including the famous Baroda carpet, studded with gems and worth thousands of pounds sterling. Then there are what may be termed "side-shows" in the form of rooms furnished by the Schools of Art at Bombay, Lahore and Madras. These contain specimens of the art industries typical of their provinces. In the beautiful Bombay room, for instance Mr. C. L. Burns has had the walls panelled with carved teak of the pattern familiar in Bombay, and in the spaces are stretched gorgeous gold *kincobs* of an old Surat design. Prominent above the panelling are two reproductions of the famous Ahmedabad windows carved in teak, and a frieze of stencilled silk designed and made in the Bombay School. The latter is quite unique work, and will probably be in large demand when it becomes more widely known. The stencilling is done on Surat silk and remarkable gradations of colour can be obtained. It is genuine art work, for its success depends upon the skill of the designer and also of the man who cuts the design. The furniture of the room is of carved blackwood and teak, the upholstering being done with brilliantly coloured *kincobs*. This feature was introduced to show native princes and others that really exquisite furniture of any typical Indian design can be made in the country, and that there is no need to call upon the London houses, as so many wealthy Indians are prone to do. The walls of the Lahore room are entirely covered by magnificent wood-carving, with little balconies, and the Madras room contains a quantity of well made and artistic furniture in addition to other pleasing features. It is close inspection which reveals the beauty of the treasures Dr. Watt has collected, and in the intervals between the chief State functions, the Art Exhibition will probably be one of the most popular resorts in Delhi.

L. E. N.

X.

THE STATE ENTRY.

December 29.

IT has been a typical Delhi day, after all; no untimely change of weather has marred the great pageant; the sun shone from an almost cloudless sky when the Viceroy and the brother of the King-Emperor entered in state the Imperial City. There was the usual cheerless dawn, pallid mist, biting air; but as the hour drew near, the city took unto itself a genial warmth, the scene was suffused with brilliant light, the shivering moments of daybreak were forgotten. Towards high noon, the great space before the Jumma Masjid, the mighty mosque that Shah Jehan erected, presented a spectacle the like of which Delhi has not witnessed for more than two decades. You look from the wide steps before the huge gate of the Masjid, towards the long line of battlemented walls of the Fort, five hundred yards away. The space between is absolutely bare, save for a few scattered trees. If you wish to know why no building remains upon it, you must consult the records of the Mutiny. Once the city extended right up to the walls of the Fort; when Delhi was recaptured by the soldiers of the Queen, the streets that had seen so much hard fighting were razed to the ground. So it comes to pass that nowadays the Fort stands alone; and thus it was that the Jumma Masjid afforded the finest coign of vantage to-day.

The road along which the procession was to pass, runs parallel with the Fort walls until it reaches a point opposite the Jumma Masjid. Then it turns sharply, and traverses the open space at an easy gradient, right up to the steps of the mosque. Those of us who were stationed there saw the whole pageant coming straight towards us up a gentle ascent. The arcades and roof of the gateway bore many distinguished English visitors, including most of Lord Curzon's personal guests. Here also were seated, in glittering uniforms, the representatives of foreign Powers, the foreign consular officers, and many other of the guests whom the Government of India have called together from the ends of the earth. The vast steps were packed with Mussulmans, many of them splendidly attired, and all waiting in dignified solemnity for the approach of the Viceroy. Upon the sides of the road leading to the mosque large stands had been erected, not mere flimsy things of wood, but solid tiers of earth held together by blocks of stone. Away beneath the trees opposite the Lahore Gate of the Fort was a row of elephants, a hundred and fifty strong, facing the road. These were the "retinue elephants" of the ruling chiefs, and a brave show they made, with their gorgeous trappings and their resplendent howdahs. At our feet, the road was lined by soldiers in the sombre uniform of the Rifles; and no corps had a prouder claim to be in Delhi to-day. Nearly four hundred Rifles, out of a total of six hundred, were killed or wounded during the siege. Halfway down the road there was a sudden change of colour, and you saw the route was edged with scarlet. For here were the men of the Gordon Highlanders, sturdy brawny fellows, hardly one without a medal. Highlanders—Gordons and Argylls—kept the road from this point as far as our line of vision, which was bounded by the Lahore Gate, extended. And if you would fill in the picture as we saw it, you must add dense crowds of natives thronging the roadside; on the right, a squalid corner of the native city protruding outwards, its ramshackle tenements swarming with people on balconies and roofs; the open space before the Fort brown and dusty, but the trees green and refreshing to the eye; beyond the tenements, a single feathery palm, the only one in the view; towards the Jumna, country thickly wooded, with two slender minarets rising heavenward; and as a background, the rose-red walls of the Fort, clear cut against the hard blue sky. It was a magnificent scene, and though the hum of countless careless voices pervaded it, you felt that not the meanest coolie in all the multitude of sightseers could fail to carry the memory of it to his dying day.

Midday drew near, and with it an air of tense expectancy settled upon the mighty throng. They were waiting for something. The hum of voices continued, but seemed to grow softer. You felt that tens of thousands of ears were listening, listening, listening for a signal. At last it came. The roar of a gun from the Fort shook the air. A battery slowly boomed forth a Royal salute. The Viceroy had alighted in the City of the Moguls.

Straightway the pent-up feelings of the patient watchers asserted themselves. Tongues were loosened and wagged freely. Then followed another period of waiting. Suddenly the guns burst forth again. Another Royal salute, this time for the Duke and Duchess of Connaught. Yet another wait, and a prolonged one. Would they never come? The sun stood high in the heavens. It was burning hot now. The troops were feeling it in their thick uniforms. Their white helmets were no longer superfluous.

A faint, almost imperceptible strain of distant music, wherein you fancy you can discern the air that makes the heart of every true Englishman throb. A little stir among the mob; a simultaneous turning of questioning faces. And there, between the elephants yonder, a peep of a solitary figure riding along the road, and through the trees a flash of lance-points and a flutter of tossing pennons. They are nearing us at last. The moment is at hand; and slowly, very slowly, the head of the procession emerges into view.

It was led by a squadron of cavalry, furnished by the 4th (Royal Irish) Dragoon Guards. Then followed that very smart battery of Horse Gunners, the "H" Battery. The last time you had seen them, they were in action on the verge of the Grand Trunk Road, the men in khaki, dusty, begrimed, unkempt, soiled by the stains of mimic warfare. Now, in their trim blue uniforms, they presented a very different picture. After them more of the 4th Dragoon Guards, three full squadrons, well-mounted soldierly men. But it was not the escort that was engrossing attention now. The guns at the Lahore Gate crashed forth again ; the strains of the National Anthem, unmistakeable this time, were borne across the Champ de Mars ; the Viceregal Standard was suddenly fluttering from the Fort flagstaff. You could hear the retinue elephants trumpeting, and see them lifting their swaying trunks aloft in salutation. A line of glittering howdahs came in sight, their gold and silver adornments blazing in the sun. The Viceroy and the Duke and Duchess were approaching.

First after the escort rode the soldierly figure of Brigadier-General Collins, who commands the Viceroy's Escort. Then came the Herald, Major Maxwell, resplendent in a tabard of silk cloth of gold, emblazoned with the Royal Arms. He was followed by twelve trumpeters, six British and six native, wearing State coats of crimson velvet covered with gold lace and embroidered with the Royal cipher. They were all riding handsome black horses, and their saddles were covered with white leopard skins. As they drew near, they played a flourish on their long silver trumpets. Next rode the Viceroy's Bodyguard, commanded by Major Grimston, in their gorgeous uniforms of scarlet and gold, mounted on the finest bay walers that the Remount Department can procure. The pick of the bays that come to India go to the Vice-regal Bodyguard, and when you have seen them you can well believe it. Perfectly schooled, well under control yet with splendid action, they went by in faultless order; and not a man bestrode them whose dark bearded face was not stern, set, impassive, as befitted his responsibilities. But the body of cavalry which attracted most attention, and aroused most enthusiasm, was the Imperial Cadet Corps, which immediately preceded the elephants. The men who had gone before might be reckoned among the finest cavalry that the British and Native Armies can boast of; but these slim handsome young Princes, whose very bearing conveyed a subtle suggestion of noble birth, were invested with the glamour that surrounds the descendants of men famous in the long roll of Indian chivalry. Their uniform was magnificent. Their spotless white frock coats were faced with the light Star of India blue, and glistened with gold embroidery. Their waists were encircled by blue Kashmiri kamarbunds with crimson tassels, and gold sword belts buckled over all. Their turbans of delicate blue bore the Corps cypher and a brilliant gold aigrette; and their black chargers—every horse was black—carried snow leopard skins over the saddles. Never has a Cavalry Corps been more strikingly attired. At their head rode their gallant old Honorary Colonel, H. H. the Maharajah of Idar, whom Englishmen will always know and admire as Sir Pratap Singh, as brave and dashing a warrior as India has ever produced. He sat his charger as easily and as firmly as any of the youths who followed in his train. His dearest wish, he has said, is to die on horseback, as a Rajput should, fighting for his King and Emperor; but those who have learned to love him for his daring spirit and his kindliness, will pray that the day may be far distant when the leaden messenger of Death dims the keen ardour of those flashing eyes. And at his heels there rode the knightly form of the young Maharajah of Jodhpur, whom the Rahtor Rajputs are proud to call their chief; and the Maharajahs of Kishengarh, Jaora, Rutlam, and Dholepur, princes whom fate has bidden to endure the cares of a ruler in the very springtime of youth; and scions of many of the noblest Houses of Hindustan. These memorable days at Delhi may have many imposing spectacles in store for us; they will have none more impressive than that of these lads, in their snow-white uniforms, joyfully participating in a ceremonial intended to do honour to the King and Emperor to whom they freely proffer allegiance.

Yet the finest sight was still to follow, for here came the elephants, lumbering along, gigantic and a little grotesque, but always ponderously stately.

You felt at once, as you looked down upon the long vista of swaying gorgeous howdahs, reared high above the crowd of spectators, dwarfing the cavalry, making all else seem puny by comparison, that in no other way could the representatives of the King-Emperor and the Royal Family have entered Imperial Delhi. And the people felt it too. You could tell that from the way their glances eagerly turned towards the enormous beasts of burden. As they drew nigh with slow, massive, irresistible tread, murmurs of admiration arose from the natives, but these quickly subsided into an awed silence. For a moment there was a death-like stillness, the multitude was stricken dumb by the amazing revelation of splendour, and then, as the Viceroy approached, cheer after cheer rent the air.

The vanguard of six elephants caparisoned exactly alike, with open silver howdahs, richly chased, was rather disregarded. They bore the Viceroy's aides-de-camp, the staff of the Duke of Connaught, the Private Secretary and Military Secretary to the Viceroy, and Mr. H. S. Barnes, Foreign Secretary and Lieutenant-Governor-Designate of Burma. But all eyes were fixed upon the two mighty elephants that followed after a little interval. The clear quick tones of a British officer rang out:—"Royal Salute! Present Arms!" The band before the steps of the mosque, which had played a flourish as the Viceroy approached, burst forth into "God Save the King." The vast concourse was standing, the English with topees raised, the troops presenting arms, the thousands of natives salaaming. And in the centre of the scene, borne upon high in a glittering howdah, an umbrella-shaped canopy—the symbol of power—held over him, sat the Viceroy, serene, dignified, with right hand uplifted, accepting the salute on behalf of his Royal and Imperial Master.

It was one of the supreme moments of a brilliant career. No honours that may in after years be conferred upon Lord Curzon, can be comparable to this, that it has been his privilege to enter Delhi, the city which race after race of valiant men has fought for, as the vicegerent of the First Emperor of all India, to proclaim to the world his Sovereign's assumption of the Imperial dignity. All the long years of laborious service for the Empire, the unseen toil, the devoted drudgery that no one save himself will ever know the full measure of, must have found their compensation in that instant's consciousness that the dramatic picture, with its setting of giant mosque and grim fortress, would live in the pages of history while the name of Britain endures. And the Viceroy looked a fitting representative of the long line of illustrious men who have won and held India for the English, as he sat there, calm and self-controlled, his face slightly flushed, his firm lips set, his head slightly inclined forward in acknowledgment, his single gesture tranquil and restrained. It was a moment to have lived for.

Lord Curzon was wearing a blue uniform, with the ribbon of the Star of India. Lady Curzon, who looked smiling and radiant, was attired in a white dress, with a lace fichu, caught on either side with bunches of real violets, both light and dark blue. She carried a white parasol, with bunches of violets painted on the panels. The elephant on which the Viceregal pair were carried was one of the finest specimens that India could provide. Its name was Luchman, and it was lent by the Maharajah of Benares. The howdah, which was that used by Lord Lytton in 1877, was a massive structure of burnished silver, bearing the Royal Arms on its sides done in gold, and with richly embossed golden edges. Its seats were upholstered in figured pink silk. The saddle-cloth or jhool was of immense size, almost covering the body of the elephant, and its gold fringes nearly swept the ground. It was stiff with heavy gold embroidery, so lavishly introduced as to almost conceal the original foundation. In the centre of the design was a representation of the sun, and on each side a lion rampant. Before the elephant, and at its sides, walked spearmen and chobdars clad in the scarlet Viceregal livery. The spearmen carried long silver spears, with golden tassels depending from the blade-hilts. Some of the chobdars bore maces surmounted by elephants' heads, all fashioned out of silver. Others carried silver staves topped by the Tudor crown.

Closely following the Viceroy came their Royal Highnesses the Duke and Duchess of Connaught, mounted on an imposing elephant named Moula

Bux, lent by the Maharajah of Jaipur. The Duke, who looked in excellent health, and contemplated the scene with intense interest, was wearing the scarlet uniform of a Field-Marshal, and the ribbon of the Star of India. Those who remember his Royal Highness during his prolonged sojourn in India commented upon his unchanged appearance. The hand of Time has dealt lightly with the soldier-son of the late Queen-Empress. The Duchess, who was also looking in the best of health and spirits, was clad in a costume of the Star of India blue, which is a pale turquoise. She had a hat to match and carried a white parasol. The Royal howdah, lent by the Maharajah of Bulrampur, was even more elaborate than that which contained the Viceroy. A large panel at its side contained a representation of an ibex, done in gold in high relief upon a background of silver. Above was a smaller panel, containing golden parrots pecking at fruits. The rest of the side was cleverly fashioned into the form of a tiger, in the act of springing upon a huddled antelope. The antelope formed the lower part of the side, at the point where it joined the front panel; and the whole was worked in gold upon silver. It was impossible to see more of its decorations as the procession slowly filed past; but one caught a glimpse of purple upholstery within. The great jhool was almost identical with the Viceroy's, and precisely the same number of attendants with silver spears and maces, were in attendance upon their Royal Highnesses.

But the Viceroy was moving forward. The pageant was passing right round the Jumma Masjid preparatory to traversing the road leading to the Chandni Chauk. Who shall describe the resplendent array that followed? Over fifty elephants marched past, with rolling, shambling gait. Princes bearing the greatest names in the Golden Book of India defiled before our dazzled vision. The whole road, right away to the walls of the Fort, was flashing with precious metals aflame in the sunlight. Not a howdah that was not covered with gold and silver. Not a jhool that was not decked in gleaming gold embroidery. Not an elephant that was not closely surrounded by gaudy spearmen, and driven by a mahout in rainbow colours. The very foreheads of the elephants were daubed with bright pigments. And the princes that they bore, who shall recount the splendour of their attire, the indescribable array of silks and satins and velvets, their flashing jewels, their ropes of pearls and necklaces of diamonds and rubies and emeralds, the splendid aigrettes in their turbans? It was a barbaric display, if you will, but it epitomised the wealth and magnificence of the immemorial East. On they came, till one almost fancied that the heavy tramp of the elephants shook the ground. The bells hanging from the howdahs clanged like cathedral chimes. Clouds of dust arose—water avails little on Delhi roads—and the uniforms of the patient troops grew soiled. But still the march went on, and the people cheered with wild enthusiasm as they passed. Never has there been such a demonstrative Indian crowd. First came the Nizam of Hyderabad on a huge elephant draped with plain yellow velvet. His howdah was also yellow, but it was quite undecorated. It was perhaps the plainest and simplest display in the whole procession, and yet it was curiously impressive, because the yellow was so deep and vivid. His Highness sat alone on the front seat of his howdah, with one member of his staff behind him. On his left rode the Maharajah of Travancore in a magnificent howdah of chased gold and silver, with a splendid canopy of the same precious metals. The Maharajahs of Mysore and Kashmir came next, then the Maharajahs of Gwalior and Jaipur, the Maharajah Holkar and the Maharajah of Bundi, and after them a long procession of the greatest chiefs in India.

At last the final elephant had disappeared around the Jumma Masjid. Let me state the bald truth at once. After the elephants had passed, the rest of the procession seemed flat and stale by comparison. As in size, so in impressiveness, the elephants dwarfed all else ; though under ordinary circumstances one would have regarded the rest of the cavalcade as a sufficing pageant enough. His Royal Highness the Grand Duke of Hesse, wearing the dark-blue ribbon of the Victorian Order, drove by, with his staff and escort of the 15th Hussars. Then came his Excellency the Governor of Bombay and Lady Northcote, with the staff, in full uniform, in carriages. And here I may note that a question as to whether the Governor of Bombay or of Madras should be given precedence arose while the arrangements for the Durbar were in progress. Precedence was claimed for Madras because it was the older province, but Lord George Hamilton decided that the question was to be settled according to the seniority of the respective heads of the two Presidencies. Lord Northcote therefore takes rank at the Durbar next to the Viceroy and the Royalties. His Excellency wore his full official uniform and the ribbon of the Order of the Indian Empire. Lady Northcote was attired in a handsome white dress with black stripes and a black hat; she carried a white parasol.

At the risk of repetition, I must again mention the Bombay Bodyguard. Every one here says that they are the finest Bodyguard in camp. They are superior in physique and soldierly appearance to the Viceregal Bodyguard, and almost equally well mounted. Followed Lord Ampthill, with Lady Ampthill and his staff and Bodyguard. The Governor of Madras is big in physique, ruddy of countenance, and a fine figure in uniform. He also was wearing the ribbon of the Order of the Indian Empire. Lady Ampthill's costume was of pink, edged with black velvet; she wore a pink hat and carried a dove-grey parasol. Sir Charles Rivaz, Lieutenant-Governor of the Punjab, passed next, by virtue of his position as ruler of the province in which the Durbar is held. And after him there rode, a solitary but commanding form, Lord Kitchener. It was curious to note the new Commander-in-Chief's absolutely immobile features. Stern, self-contained, unresponsive, you might have thought the great soldier supremely indifferent to the whole picturesque scene were it not for the sudden quick glance with which, as in a flash, his eyes swept over the crowd. He was preceded by a brilliant staff, and escorted by a squadron of Volunteer cavalry.

Need I describe in detail the dignitaries who followed, the Lieutenant-Governors and Chief Commissioners and Members of Council? They were mostly in carriages, each with his special escort of native cavalry, save only the Members of Council, who get all the hard work of a great position, without its display. We were a little weary by this time, for we had been in our positions for hours, and the strain was growing irksome. But two more features of the procession aroused our flickering interest. One was the sight of his Highness the Khan of Khelat, riding side by side with the Agent to the Governor-General in Baluchistan, followed by a retinue of wild reckless-looking Baluch chiefs on shaggy ponies. The other, Colonel Deane, the Chief Commissioner of the North-West Frontier Province, with a train of those troublesome notabilities, the Pathan chiefs, great bearded men, fearless in look and bearing, staring a little contemptuously at the obsequious people of Delhi. They included such celebrities in frontier warfare as the Mehtar of Chitral, the Nawab of Dir, and the Khan of Nawagai. Then, bringing up the rear, a forest of glancing lance points and fluttering pennons, the 11th (Prince of Wales' Own) Bengal Lancers, reputed to be the most splendid regiment of cavalry in the Indian Army. Last of all, more elephants. For here were all the retinue elephants that had saluted so solemnly when the Viceroy passed. They streamed along, a hundred and fifty of them, their howdahs packed with the retainers of the chiefs, their glowing trappings a perfect kaleidoscope of colour.

Thus did the Viceroy and the Duke and Duchess of Connaught enter Delhi. As a spectacle, it was unsurpassable. The bright sunshine, and the solemnity of the occasion, alike redeemed the procession from all suspicion of tawdriness. Shah Jehan and Aurangzeb may have had more magnificent displays, but the blending of Oriental splendour with the living embodiments of the military strength and the administrative capacity of the West, gave a touch of dramatic contrast which Delhi can never have known in the days of the Moguls.

XI.

THE JOURNALIST: A TALE OF WOE.

December 30.

I MET him at high noon in the Chandni Chauk. There was a block of traffic. Around him were ramshackle ekkas, rough bullock carts, carriages loaded with the gaudy retainers of native chiefs, stray tongas, casual police sowars. Just behind his victoria stood a lumbering coach drawn by a couple of camels. The heads of the camels were protruded over his own; but he heeded them not. He wore a frock-coat that once had been black, but was now thick with dust. There was a perceptible layer of dust over the cushions whereon he sat; dust hung on his very eyebrows, and yellowed his brown moustache. He looked the picture of resignation. The old impatient intolerance of delay, that I had known in other climates, had been wiped out of him. He had grown passive in adversity. The spirit of the country brooded over him. The East had claimed him for its own.

A faint gleam of recognition lit his eye as I shouldered my way towards him. He uttered no word of greeting; yet I saw he wanted to speak. In a dull, even voice, from which all trace of poignant emotion had vanished, he began: "There was a time when I would have been furious at this; now I tolerate it. Do you know how long I have been wedged in this infernal jam? I have been here twenty minutes. But that is nothing. Yesterday I was stuck in one place, unable to move, for over an hour. Think of it! An hour, my friend; and with columns of copy in my mind that I knew I could never put into words. You see that driver? I do not know my way about Delhi; neither does he. I do not know a word of Hindustani except *jao;* he does not recognise a word of English except d——n. I tell him to drive to some place. He starts off with cheerful alacrity, without the faintest idea where he is going; and I find myself in—this."

He cast his hands abroad despairingly. It was the first sign of animation he had shown. He was warming to his theme.

"I have been trying to call on a Maharajah. I had a letter to him. I started out clean and comparatively respectable. Now I am as you see. Look at my collar. Look at my coat. Look at the streaks of dirt on my face. I tell you they would look upon me with suspicion in the casual ward of a workhouse. This dust is awful. My throat is full of it, and my eyes, and my hair. All the water in the New River will not make me clean, all the sodas that Schweppe ever made will not wash its taste away. It is a mercy that I have a frock-coat at all. I lost a bicycle and a cabin trunk on the way up. I called yesterday on two Dukes and a Governor; and I had to wear a pair of borrowed boots, cracked right across. Here they are; look at them; I ask you, are they ducal? But it is the trouble of finding one's way about that upsets me most. These drivers know nothing. There are not half enough signboards; and at night you cannot see anything. Do you know that I have lost my way three times after dark trying to find our camp? Once I wandered about aimlessly for two hours. The other night I went to dine with the Panjandrum of Madagascar. His camp is quite close to ours, not more than four miles away. There was a thick mist. As usual, we lost our way. Then the horses started jibbing. I finished the journey on foot. I was not very late, as things go in this camp. I got there by the time they were serving the ice-pudding. Another time I borrowed a bike to go out to dinner. I managed the outward journey all right, but on the way back was misdirected. Somehow I found myself toiling up a road towards the Ridge. Then my chain broke. My dear sir, unless you have just come from Fleet Street, and found yourself in dress clothes and a covert coat, standing with a broken bicycle chain in your hand amid the freezing darkness of the Delhi Ridge at midnight, you cannot know what the blank bewilderment of utter misery really means."

The traffic was moving onward now. The road was clearing. I stepped in and sat down beside him. The slow monologue continued.

"And then there is the cold. It is all very well for you Anglo-Indians, who are accustomed to this dreadful weather."

I thought of long years spent amid the steamy heat of the South, with never a breath of chilly wind ; but I held my peace.

"I never dreamed of this, and I cannot stand it. I should think there is nothing in the world like the cold of Delhi. It is not that it is severe ; it is the quality of it that knocks you over. Dry cold in other places is invigorating and stimulating. This is a sort of dead cold, and reduces you to a clammy corpse. It creeps in everywhere ; the thickest overcoats are not proof against it. From ten in the morning to five in the afternoon I live ; then the climate is delightful. But that is just the time when I want to be out seeing things ; and when I start at night to write, my brain is congealed. It will not work, nor will my hand hold the pen. Do you know how I wrote my last letter? My servant kept replenishing a basin of hot water on the table, and I dipped my fingers into it at the end of every sentence. How can I write decently under such conditions? And this is your coral strand! Never will I grumble at the English winter again."

"But at least," I urged, "you are seeing wonderful scenes, the like of which you may never see again."

He looked at me reproachfully. "My good man," was his bitter reply, "Don't you understand that

that is just the very worst part of the whole miserable business? I cannot do them justice; no one can. Did you drive along the Chandni Chauk just before the State Entry? Yes? So did I, and I shall never forget the sight to my dying day. When I saw those great masses of people, all those amazing bright turbans, all those rich vestments, I realised at last that I was not equal to it. That extraordinary blaze of colour can never be put into mere words. How can you convey to the public at home a picture of those tens of thousands of dark impassive faces, framed in the brightest hues? The artists are just as perplexed. The black-and-white men say that without colour the whole impression is lost; the painters that no colour is equal to it. Give me a grey November day in London, a mass of dingy houses, and a mob in sombre clothes. I can do that, and make you see it. But this has shown me what I never fully realised before. There are occasions when words are impotent."

The note of despair deepened as he went on.

"And then there was that procession. Do you remember that moment just as Curzon reached the Masjid, and we looked right along that sloping road crammed with elephants? Do you remember how the whole place seemed one shining, gleaming, swaying medley of burnished gold and silver? I tell you, the splendour of that vision fairly made me gasp and catch my breath. Recollect how seasoned Anglo-Indians, used to these pageants, broke out involuntarily into ejaculations of wonder and admiration. How could I tell 'em at home about it as it ought to be told, when the dazzle of it all was still in my eyes as I sat down to write my telegram? Telegrams! A man wants to shut himself up in a room for a month to do it, and hammer out words like beaten gold. How was I to say it, with the printers waiting there in London, and only a couple of hours to do the thing? How was I to get in the view of all those glittering howdahs, and the proud Maharajahs seated on high, the note of armed strength in the troops, the note of hushed awe in the crowds; and then the setting, with that great red Fort and that mighty Masjid, and the green trees between. And all the time I knew that half the people who would read my stuff didn't know the difference between a howdah and a mahout. And there were some other things that they could never understand, and wouldn't believe if I had put 'em in. For instance, if I had said that old Sir Pratap Singh was cheered to the echo, while Kitchener was almost unrecognised and hardly cheered at all, they would have thought me mad. Why does Kitchener tilt his helmet over his eyes? He ought to have been labelled. I never spotted him myself until he was almost past. And what is the use of my saying that the Nizam did not wear a single jewel except his Order? It's no good telling 'em that he never does. Their idea of the Nizam is that he never thinks of sitting down to breakfast with less than a couple of million pounds worth of diamonds hung about him ; and when the British public get a fixed idea, you can't knock it out of 'em."

For a space he grew silent and reflective, and thoughtfully brushed his dusty sleeve. We were approaching the railway station. Suddenly he broke out again.

"There's another thing, you know. All these novel terms and expressions leave me fairly boggled. I'm afraid I get frightfully mixed up sometimes. The names and titles of the chiefs are so very confusing to the stranger. For instance, can you tell me the precise difference between the Kinkob of Ahmedabad and the Jam of Jamnagar?"

I wilted, and fled into the station.

XII.

THE GREAT DAY.

January 1.

TO-DAY, in brilliant sunshine, and with all the blazonry of pomp and circumstance, his Excellency the Viceroy and Governor-General of India proclaimed in open Durbar at Delhi the Coronation of his Most Gracious Majesty the King, Emperor of India. The ceremony was held in a vast Amphitheatre on the plain beyond the Durbar Camp, the site being that whereon Lord Lytton held the historic Imperial Assemblage of 1877. Picture a mighty structure shaped like a horse-shoe, set in the midst of a flat and bare and dusty wilderness. Within, tier after tier of seats; it was estimated that the Amphitheatre held ten thousand people. The seats were sheltered from the glare of the sun by a light roof, relieved externally by a series of miniature domes of creamy white picked out with gold. The passages were covered with crimson carpets, and in front of the lowest tier was a broad carpeted pathway which gave access to the Viceregal dais. Right opposite the entrance to the great arena, this dais jutted out prominently from the tiers. It was covered by a separate graceful domed canopy, done in white and gold, the interior of the roof of the canopy being beautifully moulded.

Upon the dais glittered the thrones of the Viceroy and the Duke of Connaught, standing on carpets heavy with gold embroidery. That of the Viceroy was of shining gold and silver. The framework of the seat and back was silver. Golden heads of lions formed the corners of the back, and between them the Star of India was emblazoned in gold upon silver, surmounted by a golden crown resting upon silver lotus leaves. The arms were fashioned into golden lions, in a standing position, with heads erect. Lions' legs, done in gold, formed the supports of the throne. It was upholstered in rich crimson velvet, as was also the massive silver footstool. The Duke of Connaught's throne was similar in general design, but not quite so richly ornamented and slightly lower. At the back of the canopy rose the Viceregal flagstaff. The arena was quite bare save for the lofty Royal and Imperial flagstaff in its centre.

The plain outside was thick with troops from an early hour in the morning. There were very nearly forty thousand on parade in review order, representing the flower of the British and Indian Armies. Before the entrance to the arena, at a distance of exactly two hundred yards, were drawn up twenty-six battalions of British and native Infantry, a solid phalanx of two Divisions facing the Amphitheatre, extending along a front of just under a thousand yards. In the rear of the Infantry Divisions were four Mountain Batteries and two companies of Sappers and Miners. On their left flank, seven battalions of Imperial Service Infantry, two companies of Sappers and Miners, and a Brigade Division of Royal Field Artillery. On their right flank, the Volunteer Infantry, three companies of Sappers and Miners, a balloon and pontoon section, six companies of the Royal Garrison Artillery, and two Brigade Divisions of the Royal Field Artillery. In a line from the extreme right flank of the Army to the Amphitheatre, and from the extreme left flank to the Durbar Road, the 3rd Bengal Cavalry, in extended order, kept the plain clear of stragglers. At the point where the Durbar Road approached the Amphitheatre, it was lined by three batteries of the Royal Horse Artillery. The Durbar Road for a distance of nearly two miles was kept by cavalry. First came fourteen squadrons of Imperial Service Cavalry; then six companies of Mounted Infantry; then the Divisional and Corps Cavalry, sixteen squadrons strong; after these the little detachment of Volunteer Cavalry; and finally, as the Amphitheatre was neared, two full Cavalry Brigades, twenty-four squadrons strong. Two other thoroughfares led to the scene of the Durbar, Prince's Road and Review Road. These were lined by the mounted retinues of the ruling chiefs. Their footmen, a motley assemblage, and the army of elephants, were massed upon the plain to the south-west of the Amphitheatre.

This, then, was the setting of the picture. The illimitable brown plain; in its centre, the great Amphitheatre, its roof gleaming in the sunshine;

beyond and around it, the King-Emperor's Army, battery after battery, squadron after squadron, battalion after battalion; and in the distance, the huge array of elephants, and the mob of retainers of the ruling chiefs. As a spectacle, it was too vast. The troops looked like casual splashes of colour on a khaki background. When they moved, you could only see their weapons flashing through clouds of dust. But the stern intimation of power was there, the sense of unquestioned control, the feeling that in these dull-hued guns, these serried ranks of hard-bitten warriors, lay the final title of the English to hold India. For the place of Durbar was literally enveloped by one great, efficient, irresistible fighting machine.

It is hard to say when the first spectators began to arrive. All were compelled to be in their places by eleven, but many of them, some enthusiastic, some nervous about being late, began to drive up far earlier. The British Infantry who formed the guards were early on duty, and duly presented arms as the chiefs and high officers entitled to salutes alighted. The arrangements for parking the carriages necessitated endless preliminary experiment and consideration. Thousands and thousands of carriages had to be parked. Perfect organisation could not be expected. The marvel was that there was not hopeless confusion.

The period of waiting was bright and warm, and previous anticipations of bleak and unpropitious weather were happily falsified. There was no lack of interesting incidents for the spectators. Shortly after ten o'clock the ruling chiefs and the heads of the various Administrations began to appear. At half-past ten the arena was crowded with people, most of the men in uniform, the ladies in dainty toilettes. For a time you were allowed to wander about, and it was wonderful how many chance acquaintances from all parts of India one met during that preliminary wait. The spectators were thickest before the seats reserved for ruling chiefs and their retinues, whose splendid attire was something to marvel at. Never has such an amazing collection of jewels of price been concentrated in one small area. Some Shan Chiefs, in dark crimson velvet, thickly spangled with gold, were particularly conspicuous. Their heads were crowned with high conical structures, fashioned of pure gold and blazing with emeralds and diamonds. Hundreds of people took snapshots of them. The camera was everywhere. It was odd to see a portly Maharajah, in a shining silver mantle over a robe of deep yellow, walking about with a hand camera photographing every striking figure he met. It is impossible to convey in mere words any true impression of the barbaric wealth that confronted you at every turn. If you see one sword scabbard encrusted with diamonds and rubies, one mantle sewn with a design of emeralds and seed pearls, one great nodding aigrette fastened with a massive brooch that millionaires might crave for in vain, one priceless necklace of diamonds of perfect purity, one resplendent figure decked out in all the magnificence of Sardanapalus, you can perhaps indicate its appearance with some degree of accuracy. But multiply these wonders a thousand times, group them in one small space, cover them with a blaze of sunshine, set them in motion, and the effect becomes indescribable.

Soon after eleven a bugle rang out and the arena was quickly cleared. All the ruling chiefs, save some belated Mussulman potentates who had stayed too long at their devotions, had arrived. The Nizam, clad in a dark-blue uniform, surmounted by a turban of yellow and wearing the ribbon of the Star of India, was in his place. Near him sat the Gaekwar of Baroda, in a white satin robe edged with gold, also wearing the riband of the Star of India; and beyond, row after row of great chiefs and nobles. At this point there was a moving incident, when amid cheers three aged native Mutiny veterans, too feeble to join in the march around the arena that was to follow, were slowly led across the open space to their seats.

At length all, save the principal figures in the great function, were in their places. All the notabilities who owe allegiance to the Supreme Ruler of India were there; princes whose subjects are numbered by millions; statesmen who have grown grey in the service of the Empire; wild Pathan chiefs from the grim frontier fastnesses; slant-eyed Shans who guard our frontiers on the remote Mekong; Arab Sultans, cloaked and hooded, who have turned from the waning Crescent of the Ottomans to the Star of India; handsome Rajput chieftains, whose features and bearing presented a better proof than the longest written pedigree of their claim of ancient descent; rough Baluchi nobles, frank-eyed and unafraid of the splendour around them; rulers from Kathiawar and Central India, clad in rich silks, decked in flashing jewels; all the glory, all the splendour, all the pride of India were epitomised in that brilliant throng. And there sat, too, the representatives of the liberty-loving colonies of Greater Britain; the chosen emissaries of the Powers; leaders of English society; knots of wide-eyed gaping tourists; many a soldier who has fought for the King, many a civilian who has slaved for him. What a wonderful revelation of colour it was! All the technique of Flaubert, all the vivid magic of Kipling, would not serve to convey in mere words a satisfying realisation of that glorious assemblage. For be it remembered that the men in ordinary morning dress were few. Uniforms or the splendid costumes of the natives predominated. The black coat of private life has been at a discount to-day. And the English ladies, in their handsome dresses, enhanced the brightness of the scene. And yet—and yet. It is the first duty of a chronicler of great events to be accurate; and it would be misrepresenting the obvious were it not said that some of the effect was lost because the bulk of the gay throng was in shadow. The scarlet uniforms in the open arena, the white and gold canopy over the dais, the glittering thrones themselves, received their due meed of sunlight; but if some wizard influence could have swept away the roof for a brief space, the effect would have been immeasurably heightened.

The massed bands in the arena—there were two thousand bandsmen, directed by a bandmaster who spoke through a megaphone—had been playing stirring tunes to beguile the period of waiting. Outside upon the plain, the Herald and his trumpeters, blazing with colours, had long since taken up their position. The "H" Battery of Royal Horse Artillery, the 1st Battalion of the Northamptonshire Regiment, and the 15th Sikhs, forming a portion of the Viceroy's escort, were drawn up near the entrance, awaiting his Excellency's arrival. But there was still nearly an hour of waiting.

Next came the most pathetic and, in some way, the most interesting incident of the whole Durbar. To the tune of "See the Conquering Hero Comes," the selected veterans of the Mutiny, European and native, slowly marched into the arena, the bands afterwards playing "Auld Lang Syne" as they fell into their allotted places. There were about forty Europeans and Eurasians, and close upon two hundred in the native ranks. White-haired, bowed with age, some faltering, but many still with firm step and eye undimmed, they advanced before the assembled multitude. And it was splendid to see them, conquering their infirmities for a few brief moments by a triumphant effort of will, tramping along with pride in their glance, almost as briskly as they did in the days of long ago, when they fought amid the roar of the guns at Delhi and Lucknow. You might search the wide world over for half a century, and never see a more moving sight than we witnessed to-day when these hoary veterans went by. Many an eye was filled with tears, many an one felt a choking in the throat. For these were the men who had helped to save India for the British ; the men who had fought for months in the fiercest heat, without whom there might have been no Durbar at all on this memorable New Year's Day. Small wonder that, as they passed, the whole vast audience rose to their feet to do them honour, as if moved by an irresistible impulse. And as they marched toward their allotted place, cheer after cheer rent the air. It was a purely spontaneous act of homage to gallantry, written in no programme, inspired by no formulated scheme. For these were not the plaudits dictated by convention ; they were the outcome of heartfelt emotion.

Suddenly, close at hand, the sound of bagpipes arose. A guard of honour of a hundred men of the 2nd Battalion Gordon Highlanders, under Major Stanton and Lieutenant Conyngham, with Lieuten ant Maitland carrying the King's colour, came marching into the arena. They were picked men of a famous regiment, every one of whom had seen service, bronzed, stalwart fellows of fine physique. Headed by pipers, fifes and drums, they tramped steadily round with fixed bayonets, and lined up smartly, confronting the dais. Another pause, and then the sound of guns without, firing a Royal Salute. A squadron of British cavalry trotted into sight beyond the eastern horn of the Amphitheatre; and then a carriage containing their Royal Highnesses the Duke and Duchess of Connaught, driven by postilions in scarlet and black velvet, drove into the arena. The escort riding proudly before them was a squadron of the 9th Lancers. Cheers went up as the Lancers trotted by, swelling into a roar of applause as the Duke and Duchess approached the dais. The guard of honour presented arms and the massed bands played the National Anthem. The whole assemblage rose and remained standing. The carriage paused for a moment before the dais until the strains had died away. Then their Royal Highnesses, who were received by Sir Hugh Barnes, the Foreign Secretary, and his staff, alighted and ascended to the dais. The Duke took his seat upon the throne set apart for him, and the Duchess seated herself upon one of the two chairs behind the thrones. The Duke was wearing the full uniform of a Field-Marshal, with the ribbon of the Order of the Indian Empire and the collar of the Star of India. His breast was covered with orders and in his right hand he held his Marshal's bâton. Her Royal Highness was attired in a pale yellow-brown costume and wore a hat trimmed with cream roses. She was wearing several orders. When she first arrived her dress was covered with a light grey mantle. As the Duke sat upon his throne, his sword lightly resting on the footstool his feet scorned to use, his bâton on his thigh, he looked a splendid and knightly figure, a princely soldier worthy to be the centre of that mighty throng.

Yet another wait of a few minutes. Then you saw bayonets flashing along the lines of troops on the plain, as they came to the salute. The 4th Dragoon Guards came into sight, and formed up immediately outside the Amphitheatre. Followed the Viceregal Bodyguard in scarlet, passing at a walking pace around the arena, keeping rank perfectly. After them, the Imperial Cadet Corps, in their magnificent white uniforms, the aigrettes on their splendid turbans glistering as they passed. And lastly, the Viceregal carriage, with gallant Sir Pratap Singh, the Honorary Colonel of the Imperial Cadets, riding on its left on a coal-black charger, and Major Grimston, the Commandant of the Body-guard, on its right. Cheering began as the carriage entered, and all present rose to their feet. And when the Viceroy had traversed half the distance to the dais, the guns outside commenced to boom forth another Royal Salute, the Viceregal Standard was unfurled from the flagstaff behind the central canopy, and the massed bands once more played the National Anthem. You could see the 4th Dragoon Guards and the 11th Bengal Lancers outside, trotting into position at their appointed place. The Imperial Cadets were already hurriedly dismounting at the verge of the arena, and forming up to march to their seats at the rear of the dais. But no one heeded them. The gaze of all was fixed upon Lord Curzon as he alighted, calm and dignified, and walked up the steps of the dais, followed by Lady Curzon. His Excellency was in full political uniform, with the ribbon of the Order of the Indian Empire and the collar of the Star of India. Lady Curzon was wearing a lovely dress of the pale Star of India blue, with a hat trimmed with light-blue wisteria flowers. The Viceroy was received at the top of the steps by Sir Hugh Barnes, Sir Walter Lawrence and several aides-de-camp. As he passed beneath the canopy he saluted and bowed to the Duke of Connaught, who had risen when the National Anthem commenced. The Duke, who remained standing before his throne, saluted and bowed in return, and gave a deeper bow as Lady Curzon passed to her seat. The Viceroy having saluted the Duchess of Connaught, turned and faced the audience, bowing slightly to the vast throng on his right and left. All four continued standing for the space of perhaps a minute; then the Viceroy turned and spoke to the Duke, the Duke saluted, and both took their seats. There was a pause, which seemed minutes rather than seconds, while the cannon on the plain roared out the rest of the salute. The Viceroy, collected and impassive, was the cynosure of every eye. Then, when the Imperial Cadets, headed by the Maharajah of Idar, had passed to their seats amid cheers, when the last gun had resounded in the still air, the tall figure of Sir Hugh Barnes was seen walking to the front of the dais. He halted before the Viceroy, bowed profoundly, and preferred an inaudible request. He bowed again, faced the arena, and signalled to the bandmaster. There was a long deep roll from the drums, sharp piercing notes from the bugles, a final loud outburst of stirring music. The massed bands were sounding a summons to the Herald. The Durbar had begun.

From the plain there floated the sweet clear tones of silver trumpets. Then right before the entrance to the arena appeared the Herald on a great black charger, looking almost gigantic as he paused there in the full sunlight. He was followed by twelve trumpeters, six British and six native, all riding fine black horses. The trumpeters sounded another flourish, and then advanced at a walk into the arena. The Herald and six trumpeters rode around one side, and the drummer and six trumpeters traversed the other side. The two sections, their horses in perfect control, formed up in front of the guard of honour, facing the Viceregal dais, the Herald standing before them and saluting. They presented a splendid appearance. The Herald was Major A. G. Maxwell, of the 6th (Prince of Wales') Bengal Cavalry, a nephew of Lord Roberts, and an officer with a commanding presence. He was wearing a white helmet with a gold and white puggaree. His burly figure was resplendent in a rich satin tabard bearing the Royal Standard on front and back, and on each sleeve. The lions on the sleeves were worked in cloth of gold, and the whole tabard was elaborately embroidered. White breeches and jack-boots completed the uniform. In his right hand, the butt resting on his thigh, he held a heavy mace of ebony and silver, surmounted by a silver crown. His saddle was covered with a white leopard skin, and from his horse's head-collar there hung a long red-and-white plume. The British trumpeters wore white helmets, and the natives white puggarees edged with gold. They were clad in coats similar to those worn in the Household Cavalry Band, of dark crimson velvet, covered with stripes of gold lace. The Royal and Imperial cipher, "E. R. I." was embroidered on the front and back of the coats. Their saddles were also covered with white leopard skins. From their trumpets hung satin banderoles bearing the Royal Arms; and the drums were decked with satin drum banners similarly adorned.

Once more the silver trumpets sounded a flourish. Then the Viceroy, leaning slightly forward, commanded the Herald to read the Proclamation announcing the Coronation of his Majesty the King, Emperor of India. Not a sound was audible throughout the whole vast assemblage as he wheeled his horse round, and faced the entrance to the arena. In a loud voice, audible in every part of the Amphitheatre, he slowly declaimed the stately Proclamation. Wheeling again, he once more faced the Viceroy. For the fourth time the trumpets rang out a flourish. As their last notes died tremulously away, the great Royal Standard was unfurled from the central flagstaff, the guard of honour presented arms, the massed bands played the National Anthem, and the entire audience rose to its feet.

That was the supreme moment of the ceremony. The sunshine touched the Viceregal canopy and flashed upon the burnished thrones, before which stood the brilliant figures of the Viceroy and the Duke of Connaught. The Amphitheatre was a blaze of colour, of glittering jewels, of gorgeous dresses. The arena was filled with uniforms. Men of all races and hues, the greatest and noblest and most famous in India, joined in one spontaneous act of homage to the mighty potentate who rules over Hindustan, and whose writ runs to the farthest corners of the earth, the uttermost isles of the sea. And the central figure of the glittering throng was an English nobleman, still with the vigour and freshness of youth in face and bearing, meet representative of the Royal and Imperial Master whose humble servant he is. You thought once more of all his toil for the Empire, the years of incessant work and travel, those secret studies which were the sunken pillars on which the shining structure of his fame reposes. You thought of his first advent into India as a quiet traveller, and of the contrast as he stood there, the chosen instrument of his King and Emperor, the moving spirit of the greatest solemnity the Orient has ever witnessed. But the dominating feeling, the point upon which every portion of the ceremonial was focussed, the preponderant consciousness which no one could lose for a moment, was that the whole glowing pageant was full of the influence of the absent monarch for whose exaltation it was held. You saw it in the tens of thousands wearing the King's coat, in the gay colours and tabards bearing the King's arms, in the reverence with which the multitude greeted the King's name; you heard it in the thunder of the King's guns, in the solemn strains of the King's Anthem, in the resounding cheers which afterwards greeted the King's Message. Even the Viceroy, you remembered, counted for naught, save by the gracious favour of the King-Emperor. Viceroys come and go. They are raised on high for a brief space, and disappear. The King-Emperor remains, the constant recipient of the loyal allegiance of countless millions, endowed with the unchangeable prerogatives of Royal descent. And that was why, although the Viceroy was the leading figure, one felt the full significance of the presence of the Duke of Connaught, the brother of the Sovereign, invested with no adventitious attributes, but in very truth a Royal Prince indeed.

The booming of guns on the plain without, firing an Imperial Salute. A sound like a sharp peal of thunder, rising and falling, rising and falling; the troops were firing a *feu-de-joie*. The salute took some time to complete. At intervals, the massed bands discoursed appropriate selections. But this period was, on the whole, the most pronounced pause in the long ceremonial. At length the tale of 101 guns was complete. The Herald and trumpeters, who had retired to the entrance to the arena when the Royal Standard was hoisted, sounded another flourish. Lord Curzon, rising from his throne, addressed the Durbar.

His Excellency stood for a moment before the throne, his right hand holding a page of notes, his left foot resting on his footstool, his left hand on his thigh; there was a slight pause, then he began in slow measured tones, audible throughout the Amphitheatre, the speech which every one was eagerly expecting. To speak frankly, it was a little disappointing. Lord Curzon has accustomed Indian audiences to so high a standard of oratory that perhaps our anticipations were unduly exalted. It must be admitted that there were unusual difficulties which militated against an oratorical triumph. There was the strain of making the voice carry over a wide area. There was, perhaps, something of the feeling that most writers here have had, that words are inadequate to do full justice to the occasion. Above all, there was the absorbing interest created by the long and gracious Message from his Majesty the King-Emperor himself, which necessarily made the Viceregal pronouncement rather flat by comparison. Still, the fact remains that the Viceroy's speech contained fewer of the striking phrases and thoughts and images that one has grown accustomed to expect from him on great occasions. He wore his hat while delivering it, except when reading the King's Message, when he paused and removed it. To read about the action and gesture may seem simple and natural enough; but, as one saw them there was a peculiar impressiveness about them, conveying with the utmost emphasis the deep respect in which such a Message, at once so regal, so gracious, and so kindly, should be held. Loud cheers arose at various passages. The reference to "my dear brother, the Duke of Connaught" was the signal for a tremendous outburst of applause, which the Duke acknowledged by saluting. The announcement that the Prince and Princess of Wales were about to visit this country was received with equal enthusiasm, as was his Majesty's intimation of the gladness with which he would have visited India and held the Durbar himself, had it been possible. Lord Curzon's announcement of the benefactions which Government are about to bestow did not arouse much emotion. It is difficult, perhaps, for a race not usually demonstrative to rise to heights of ecstasy over promises of benefits which will be conferred "if circumstances permit," or over prospective boons the nature of which they are left to guess. But for all that there was no lack of hearty applause at the closing portions of the Viceroy's speech, and he resumed his seat amid a perfect roar of cheers.

The acclamations had scarcely subsided when the Herald and trumpeters again entered the arena, this time at a quick trot. They formed up before the dais. Once more the melodious notes of silver trumpets. Then Major Maxwell, swiftly turning and facing the audience, raised himself in his stirrups, waved his helmet aloft, and shouted in stentorian tones :—"Three cheers for the King-Emperor!" The effect was magical. Ten thousand people rose to their feet, and gave three long, hearty cheers for the first Emperor of All India. And even as the echo of their voices died away, the sound of distant cheering arose from the troops on the plain outside. The massed bands played the National Anthem again, after which the Herald and trumpeters trotted out of the arena, and were seen no more.

Afterwards followed the ceremony of the presentation of the ruling chiefs to the Viceroy and the Duke of Connaught. They advanced in turn to the front of the dais, and the presentations were made by Sir Hugh Barnes. The Viceroy shook hands with each ruler as he offered through him his congratulations to the King-Emperor ; the Duke of Connaught, who stood on his left, did likewise. Only the principal chiefs were presented, and this portion of the ceremony was not unduly prolonged. It was impressive to see the young Maharajahs who are enrolled in the Imperial Cadet Corps standing before the dais in their magnificent uniforms, presenting the hilts of their swords in token of fealty. The Begum of Bhopal, deeply veiled, laid a casket at Lord Curzon's feet as she was presented. After the last chief had passed,

Sir Hugh Barnes stood before the throne once more, and requested permission to close the Durbar, which was duly accorded.

Then the Viceroy departed with the same ceremonies as had attended his arrival. One of the most striking pictures of the whole Durbar was that presented as his Excellency entered his carriage. The National Anthem was resounding once more, the first guns of the final salute were reverberating. There stood the Duke of Connaught, an erect, punctilious, chivalrous figure, looking every inch of him a soldier and a prince, his heels together, his attitude rigid, his right hand raised to his helmet, saluting the representative of the King-Emperor. The Viceroy's carriage slowly moved out of the arena, the people cheering as it passed. Then the Duke relaxed his ceremonious attitude. His Royal Highness and the Duchess turned, and both bowed with unstudied ease and grace on the right hand and on the left. It was an action that looked entirely spontaneous and unpremeditated, but those who witnessed it will never forget that moment. The mighty audience was aflame with enthusiasm in an instant. With one accord thousands and thousands rose, and a deafening roar of applause went up. One thing the Durbar has shown is the enormous popularity of the Royal Family in India. Every reference to the King-Emperor, every allusion to the Duke and Duchess of Connaught, was cheered again and again. And when the Duke and Duchess departed they received a tremendous ovation.

The Grand Duke of Hesse, the Governors of Bombay and Madras, the Lieutenant-Governors, and the foreign representatives followed. Then the assembly broke up, and there was a wild rush for carriages. The Great Durbar, which had engrossed the thoughts of all India for many months, was over at last.

With the roar of guns, the strains of music, and the "long waves of acclamation" still ringing in one's ear, it is too soon to seek to assess its full significance. But it may be said that throughout its long and imposing ceremonial, it consistently revealed and expressed its main purpose, the loyal recognition by the princes and peoples of India of the gracious Ruler in whose hands their destinies rest. The British have brought the land peace. They have conferred the priceless boon of personal security. They have firmly enforced the guiding principles of law and order. They have inflexibly adhered to the loftiest maxims of justice. Throughout their administration, with all its blots and shortcomings, there has run a spirit of the truest altruism. They have shown that if conquest confers privileges it also imposes responsibilities. They have held on high a new conception of the burden of empire which the more civilised nations have not failed to recognise and to accept. But the central note of to-day's Durbar lay not so much in the justification of British rule in India, or in the admission and acceptance of its achievements by the Indian peoples. Those are issues which time alone can settle, upon which history must make the final pronouncement. The true significance of the gathering lay in its fresh revelation of the profound influence the Throne exerts over the mind and imagination of this Oriental nation. It should teach England that India requires, and must always have, a personal ruler. The people look, not to his Ministers and advisers, not even to his direct representative, but to the King-Emperor himself, as the final arbiter of their future, as the fountain of honour, as the protector of their well-being. First and last, it is loyalty to the British Crown that binds India to England, and that was the dominating spirit of to-day's unprecedented Assemblage.

XIII.

GOLDEN SHOWERS.

January 3.

LAST night was the people's night. The masses of Delhi, and the crowds of humble folk whom these festivities have drawn to the Imperial City, were allowed to wander whither they would without let or hindrance. As night fell they streamed in thousands towards the great open space between the Jumma Masjid and the Fort. They swarmed on the steps of the mosque. They were packed in dense crowds around the *maidan*. They filled the roads converging upon the scene of the great display. They covered every roof top, crammed every balcony, and clung to every tree which afforded a possible coign of vantage. The whole area was surrounded by an excited, good-humoured, noisy, chattering throng. Until last night one thought that nothing delighted the Orient so much as elephants. Now it is clear that if the inhabitants of an English village crave for circuses, the people of India revel in nothing so much as fireworks.

Let me try to convey an impression of the scene as it was revealed when the first radiance of coloured fires drove darkness away for a while. In the foreground the giant mosque, its arcades and the roofs of its surrounding wall crowded with the guests of the Viceroy and the Government, its steps holding a multitude of Mussulmans. In the left cupola, clearly visible to the sightseers, sat the Viceroy and the Duke and Duchess of Connaught and many notable men and women. The building was outlined by rows of tiny lamps. All round, as far as the eye could see, swarm upon swarm of eager spectators. You looked to the left far over the illuminated city. Nothing but a sea of people met the gaze. The whole of Delhi had turned out to see the show. This was its night of nights, the one spectacle that drew countless beholders. Wherever your glance roved there was the same array of upturned faces. The hum of innumerable voices filled the air. No longer was Delhi an awed onlooker at the stupefying splendour of pageantry. The crowd burst into roars of delight as the successive marvels of the pyrotechnist's art were lit up before them. It was a wondrous scene; and as its background you saw the massive walls of the Fort picked out in myriads of lamps, and glowing a bright red in the dazzling brilliance of the showers of gorgeous stars.

Brock for once surpassed his greatest triumphs. Probably India has never seen a more magnificent display of fireworks. They extorted admiration from the most jaded and cynical onlooker. Every conceivable kind of rocket and shell and cloud of stars was in turn exhibited. There were rockets which exploded at an enormous height and emitted clouds of white stars, which irradiated the whole landscape with silvery light. There were others that let loose hundreds of coloured stars shining like jewels. And as they slowly fell to earth they burst in their turn, and shed fresh groups of stars. Even when the stars were fading there remained in the sky showers of golden rain that lingered long and seemed loth to dwindle into evanescence. There were flights of shells that burst in mid-air and released streams of stars that slowly changed from old gold to bright red and green and blue and vivid yellow. There were bombs that stood upon the ground and sent heavenwards fiery balls of brilliant hues. There were great rockets that exploded on high like thunderbolts. There were cascades of silver fire and golden-fire, weird contrivances that whirled and whistled in mid-air, fiery snakes that writhed. But as the last delicate feature of each came the soft mild light of the showers of golden rain.

And then there were the set pieces, strange devices showing radiant diamonds, glittering suns, chromatic revolving wheels, gigantic chrysanthemums, mystic fountains and roaring Niagaras. There were clever portraits of the Viceroy and Lady Curzon, the Duke and Duchess of Connaught, and Lord Kitchener. Finally, as the chief attraction of the whole display, there were monster portraits of the Emperor and Empress. How the tens of thousands of people cheered again and again as they looked upon them! And at the end, one last overpowering revelation, when a whole thousand of white, red and blue rockets were simultaneously discharged and soared upwards, bathing the whole city in a momentary glow.

It is hard to say whether the fireworks or the crowd were the most interesting. People who were content to witness the display from the Ridge aver that it looked best from that distant standpoint. They missed the marvellous throng, and they missed the wonderful spectacle of the Chandni Chauk and the gates of the city ablaze with illuminations. But, on the other hand, they missed the discomforts of the appalling rush for conveyances after the last flight of rockets. I left my carriage hopelessly blocked in the Chandni Chauk in charge of a friend who promised to see it parked. In four hours he was unable to move five yards, and at one in the morning he was peacefully slumbering in its comfortable recesses, not having seen a single firework. The masses of carriages in the darkness on the *maidan*, the mob of escorts of the ruling chiefs, the innumerable lamps, the shouting and the yelling and the clouds of dust that enveloped everything, constituted the most amazing sight of all. But I and my companions contemplated it with tired eyes. For the best part of two hours we searched for our conveyance in vain. At last, wandering miserably about the city, we found a wretched shigram. Even then our troubles were not over, for we had literally to drag the jibbing ponies into the darkness of the Ridge. It was nearly two o'clock when we reached our camp, and it says something for the magnificence of the display, that tired and weary and frozen though we were, we all agreed that it had been well worth the toil and trouble we had endured.

XIV.

THE INVESTITURE.

January 4.

THERE was bound to come a time in the succession of brilliant spectacles which constitute this Imperial Assemblage when the eye was satiated with colour, the mind bewildered by interminable pageantry, the ordinary medium of expression exhausted by the excess of splendour upon which superlatives had been expended in lavish profusion. Some of us, I fancy, felt that this point had been reached last night as we gazed upon the magnificent scene in the Diwan-i-Am, where was held the ceremony of the Investiture of the new recipients of the Orders of the Star of India and the Indian Empire. Even the flexible and abundant English language has its limits. So, too, has the patience of readers, who must be growing wearied of adjectival narratives. If, therefore, this account of the Investiture is restrained and unemotional, it must not be assumed that the ceremony failed to fulfil the great expectations formed concerning it. Rather is the restraint a concession to those upon whom a series of glowing descriptions must be beginning to pall. Perhaps, too, a quieter vein would more correctly reproduce the sentiments of the majority of those present at the function. Nothing could exceed the magnificence of the two ceremonies of the State Entry and the Durbar. You felt they were the final triumph of the picturesqueness of the Orient and the majesty of the West united in effective combination. After them nothing could fill the imagination or satisfy the eye more completely. And so those of us—a limited number out of the multitude now assembled at Delhi—who were privileged to attend the Grand Chapters of the two great Indian Orders were interested and pleased beyond measure, but withal a little jaded.

Let me say at once that the daring experiment of doubling the size of the Diwan-i-Am, or Hall of Public Audience, where Shah Jehan and Aurangzeb sat on high in state, was in the event attended by pronounced success. Those who saw it first when the additions were in process of construction, and who contemplated them with some amount of dubiety, were compelled to admit once again that the projects of the Viceroy have been amply vindicated. There was nothing to offend the artistic susceptibilities, little even to indicate which was real and which was not. Picture a great hall built of red sandstone, supported by massive engrailed arches and clustered columns. It was lit by the electric light, but its remotest vistas were dim with the faint mist that had penetrated from without. At its farthest end was the great white marble recess, with its panels of pietra dura work bearing representations of birds and foliage, once glittering with jewels, now less gorgeous but hardly less imposing. Before the recess, on a marble platform bathed in a flood of bright light, gleamed the thrones of the Viceroy and the Duke of Connaught, with their massive silver framework, their golden lions and their richly chased ornamentation. The approach to the dais was carpeted in crimson covered with great rugs heavy with gold embroidery. As a setting for a great solemnity the scene could hardly have been surpassed.

How can one describe afresh the kaleidoscopic effects that were unfolded as the innumerable notables began to arrive? There were uniforms everywhere. All the regiments in the British and Indian Armies seemed to be represented. Then there were all the political officers, resplendent in their richly embroidered blue full dress, and the members of the various branches of the Administration—many of them wearing orders—and the diplomatic and consular representatives in full ceremonial attire, their breasts covered with decorations. And the Maharajahs, the ruling chiefs and their attendants, each one vieing with the rest in gorgeousness of costume. One marvelled at the lavishness of their jewels, their necklaces of diamonds and pearls and emeralds, their splendid sword hilts, their flashing aigrettes. One wondered how many millions of pounds were gathered together in that great red hall with its solid arches. But when one thought of the impossible task of recounting once more that vision of wealth beyond computation, of colour that would have dimmed the radiance of the unpainted visions of Titian, of stateliness such as the barbaric displays of the Moguls can never have known, one felt overwhelmed by a sense of impotence. It was something to have seen, something that will form a fadeless memory. But to write about it afterwards! I can only confine myself to a plain record of what happened.

There were many interesting incidents prior to the advent of the first procession of Knights and members of the Orders. One of these was the entrance of the Imperial Cadet Corps, whose pale blue turbans formed a refreshing contrast to the more glaring colours around them. The boy Maharajah of Patiala, a handsome child with a frank open countenance, attracted much attention. So did the stalwart native aides-de-camp to the Viceroy, big bearded men in scarlet, manifestly pleased at the conspicuous place they occupied in the gathering. And then there were the dresses of the English ladies of rank and fashion, who lent so much grace and beauty to the scene. Where all were so brilliant, it would be invidious to particularise; but space must be found to mention two. One is Lady Ampthill, whose tall graceful figure, in a dress of perfect design, covered by a rich white satin mantle embroidered with a floral pattern done in silk, was a general object of admiration, as her Excellency advanced to her seat near the dais. The other was the stately Duchess of Portland, in a dress of white satin trimmed with white tulle. Her

Grace wore a collar of pearls and diamonds. Her dark hair was wreathed with green leaves studded thickly with diamonds. Upon the shining tiaras and necklaces and the handsome dresses worn by many other ladies I am unable to dilate. Lord Kitchener, who arrived early, and looked in excellent health, was seated on the right of the dais near the Duke and Duchess of Portland. The Duke of Portland, who wore a scarlet uniform, towered prominently above most of the other men present. The other guests of the Viceroy followed in quick succession. Then there was a pause, during which the band in the gallery played a selection of stirring music. Then His Royal Highness the Grand Duke of Hesse, in a blue uniform faced with scarlet, entered the hall, followed by his suite, and took his seat on the left of the chair reserved for Lady Curzon. Suddenly the whole audience rose. The Duchess of Connaught and Lady Curzon had appeared, and were slowly walking towards the dais, followed by a train of aides-de-camp and officials. Her Royal Highness was wearing a dress of sea green satin veiled with silver embroidered lace, with flowing lace sleeves and a collar of large pearls with diamond bars. Her high coiffure was crowned with a diamond tiara. Her Excellency was in a light blue dress of heavy duchesse satin, simply made in clinging lines with a garniture of antique lace, and flowing sleeves with diamond bands on the shoulders. Her hair was coiffed low, and was crowned by an exquisite diamond coronet. Her neck was encircled with diamonds. The Duchess ascended the dais first, and Lady Curzon was seated on her left.

At length all was ready for the opening of the Chapter. The hall was filled save the vacant seats down its centre, which were reserved for the members of the two Orders. The commanding form of the Herald, Major Maxwell, wearing his tabard and carrying his baton, was seen entering. In a loud voice he commanded silence and directed all present to remain seated. His trumpeters played a flourish on their silver trumpets. Then the curtain at the entrance was lifted, and the imposing procession entered to the strains of a march played by the band. First came Mr. J. B. Wood, Under-Secretary in the Foreign Department, and Mr. Dane, Officiating Foreign Secretary. After them walked Sir Hugh Barnes, the Secretary of the Orders, wearing the mantle and badge of the Star of India. And here mention must be made of the serene dignity with which Sir Hugh Barnes has fulfilled the manifold ceremonial duties which have fallen to his lot during the many trying functions of this memorable Assemblage. Time and again he has had to play a prominent part in impressive ceremonies with the eyes of thousands fixed upon him. He has never failed to carry out his duties with a certain courtly stateliness, a calm and unfaltering demeanour, which deeply impressed all who keenly watched him. Upon Sir Hugh Barnes has fallen the main responsibility of organising this enormous gathering and of attending to its multitudinous details. He is the one man who has made no mistakes, committed no errors of judgment or taste, never failed to be ready and alert at the most trying and difficult moments. And the whole camp rejoiced this morning at the unexpected announcement that by special command of the King-Emperor the Duke of Connaught had decorated him with the Knight Commandership of the Victorian Order. Probably no other man has ever had the signal honour of being invested with knighthoods in two Orders in a single evening ; but Sir Hugh Barnes, one of the most capable administrators who has ever adorned the Indian Administration, richly deserves the distinctions he has received.

After him walked the Companions of the Order of the Indian Empire and the Companions of the Order of the Star of India. They included many men who have done good work for Great Britain in this country. Then came the Knights Commanders of the Indian Empire, among them his Excellency Sir E. Galhardo, Governor-General of Portuguese India, and the Hon'ble Sir Muncherjee Bhownaggree; and after them the Knights Commanders of the Star of India, among whom were the Sultan of Lahej, the Nawab of Junagadh, the Thakore Saheb of Palitana, and the familiar figure of Sir Edward Buck, who revisits with unfailing regularity the country in which he did so much valuable work. The Knights Grand Commanders of the Indian Empire, who came next, were each followed by two attendants. They wore the fine mantle of their rank in the Order, of dark blue lined with light blue. They were led by his Highness the Aga Khan, the most recent addition to the grade, and prominent among them were his Excellency Lord Northcote, the Thakore Saheb of Gondal, the Khan of Khelat, and the Rao of Cutch. Then came eleven Knights Grand Commanders of the Star of India in mantles of turquoise blue lined with white, headed by the gallant Maharajah of Idar. They included the Maharajahs of Rewa, Gwalior, Kolhapur, Kashmir, Travancore, and Jaipur, followed in strict order of precedence by the Gaekwar of Baroda, the Nizam of Hyderabad, and the Maharajah of Nabha. After these came the martial figure of his Royal Highness the Duke of Connaught in a military uniform, wearing the robe and insignia of the Order, and attended by the little Raja Sahib of Dholpur and the son of the Thakur of Dilwara, who acted as pages. His Royal Highness was followed by an imposing staff. Finally, there walked two aides-de-camp to the Viceroy, his Excellency's Military and Private Secretaries, and then the Grand Master of the Order himself, wearing his handsome robes and insignia. His Excellency was also attended by two pages—Mian Hari Singh, son of the Maharajah of Kashmir, and Sahibzada Hamidulla Khan, youngest son of her Highness the Begum of Bhopal. He was followed by three British aides-de-camp, two native aides-de-camp, and by Colonel Fenn, the Surgeon to the Viceroy. It should be explained that as the members of the Orders reached the dais they filed off right and left to their seats, which were duly arranged in order of precedence. As the Grand Master ascended the dais the massed bands burst forth into the National Anthem, and the entire audience, in accordance with previous instructions, rose and remained standing. The spectacle, as the Grand Master seated himself upon his throne, was magnificent. The lights had been so cleverly arranged that his Excellency and the Duke of Connaught, her Royal Highness and Lady Curzon, the Grand Duke of Hesse, and the three rows of resplendent aides-de-camp who were also on the dais, sat in an absolute blaze of illumination. Below them were grouped the great princes of the Indian Empire and the men who had won distinction in the Administration, each in his graceful mantle. And beyond row upon row of notables of the Orders, each wearing his insignia.

The Chapter immediately opened, and the ceremony of investiture began. Sir Hugh Barnes, stepping before the dais and bowing low, announced that there were one Knight Grand Commander, twelve Knights Commanders, and fourteen Companions of the Most Exalted Order of the Star of India to be invested with the insignia of their respective classes. He then delivered to the Grand Master the Sovereign's grant conferring on the

Maharajah of Cochin the dignity of a Knight Grand Commander. His Highness, attended by Sir Hugh Barnes, Mr. Wood, and by the two junior Knights Commanders, Sir James La Touche and Sir J. Price, was then conducted to the front of the dais, where he made an appropriate obeisance to the Grand Master. Sir Hugh Barnes read the Sovereign's grant. The Maharajah was then conducted to a table at the side of the dais, where Sir James La Touche decorated him with the riband and badge, and Sir J. Price attached the star of the Order to his breast. Both Knights next robed his Highness with the mantle of the Order, after which he once more proceeded to the front of the dais and made another reverence. The Under-Secretary took from the table the collar of a Knight Grand Commander, placed it upon a cushion of Star of India blue, and delivered it to the Grand Master with a low bow. His Excellency, remaining seated, invested his Highness with the collar, and in a clear voice, audible throughout the hall, addressed him as follows:—"In the name of the King, Emperor of India, I hereby invest you with the honourable insignia of the Order of the Star of India, of which Most Exalted Order his Majesty has been graciously pleased to appoint you to be a Knight Grand Commander." His Highness made another reverence, and was then conducted by Sir Hugh Barnes to his appointed seat.

The next process was the investiture of the Knights Commanders, who were conducted to the dais in groups of four. Colonel Barr, Mr. Ibbetson, Admiral Drury, Mr. Winterbotham, Mr. Monteath, Colonel Robertson, Mr. Andrew Fraser, and Mr. Barnes were in turn created Knights Bachelors of the United Kingdom. They knelt one by one before the Grand Master, who borrowed a sword from an aide-de-camp, touched the recipient of the honour lightly upon each shoulder with the naked blade, and in an impressive voice, pronounced the words "Rise, Sir James," or whatever the Christian name of the new Knight happened to be. The two Knights Commanders in attendance then invested the recipients with the Star of the Order, and they were appropriately addressed by the Grand Master, who afterwards invested each with the pale blue riband and badge. They then retired to their seats, stepping backwards and bowing low. The new Companions were afterwards conducted in groups of five to the front of the dais, and their badges, which were successively handed to Sir Hugh Barnes by the Grand Master, were duly attached. This closed the business of the Chapter, and all present rose and remained standing as the Viceroy and the Duke of Connaught withdrew from the hall amid a great array of officials, to the strains of a grand march.

Afterwards there was a Grand Chapter, at which three Knights Grand Commanders, eighteen Knights Commanders, and twenty-six Companions of the Most Eminent Order of the Indian Empire were invested. The processions and the procedure were very much the same as in the previous Chapter. The Maharajah of Sirohi, the Maharajah of Travancore, and the Maharajah of Nabha were made Knights Grand Commanders. The new Knights Commanders included Sir Lawrence Jenkins and Sir Walter Lawrence. Among the new Companions were Major Cox, Colonel Loch, Mr. Beauchamp, the Khan of Dir, the Mehtar of Chitral, the Mir of Hunza, the Rajah of Nagar, Mr. Saunders, and Mr. Faridoonji Jamshedji. Finally, the imposing procession left the hall for the last time. The ceremonies lasted until midnight. They grew a little wearisome towards the close, owing to the necessity for constant repetition in the procedure; but the function was solemn and impressive.

XV.

AN OFF DAY.

January 5.

YOU must not suppose that processions and great state ceremonies are every day occurrences. We have our quiet days in camp, when the exhausted sightseer seeks a little mild recreation and gains strength for the next big function. Such a pause we have experienced to-day. The Viceroy, Lord Kitchener, and the Governor of Madras have taken large parties to the Kutab Minar, fourteen miles away. There is an air of relaxation and of rest about the camps. You can sit before your tent door and prophesy evil regarding the ominous clouds which are threatening the overdue rain ; if you get up sufficiently early you may by dusk have succeeded in booking a berth in a special train leaving in a fortnight's time. For getting into Delhi will be put a pleasant joke compared with getting out again—but this is a story which will be told a week or so hence.

Calling is one of the features of an off day. You make an early start with a well-horsed gharry, a map, and a Camp Directory, and, if the fates are kind, you may make several calls before dinner time. The amusement has in it the spice of adventure. You go forth into the unknown, and the hour of your return no man can say. It is said that an officer went out yesterday announcing his intention of visiting the Bombay chiefs and the camp of the Gaekwar of Baroda. He has not been seen since. Calling in the Central Camp is less difficult. The books of Lord and Lady Curzon, the Duke and Duchess of Connaught and the Grand Duke of Hesse are in a *shamiana* in the grounds of the Circuit House, and the number of callers is often so great that there is quite a struggle around them. In every camp there are strange gharries and visitors making frantic endeavours to find the tents of their friends.

But on such a day the real centre of attraction is the polo ground. It is the Clapham Junction and the Row of the Durbar. There you see everybody who is anybody; there you meet friends you imagined were in London or Timbuctoo, or anywhere except in Delhi. Morning and afternoon comes the same throng, every road with its unending line of traffic; visitors afoot, visitors on horses, visitors in tongas, in landaus, in drags, in rickshaws, in camel carriages, in every conceivable vehicle. It is for afternoon tea at the polo ground that the ladies reserve their most enchanting dresses and their most obstructive hats. It is to the polo ground that everyone sooner or later makes his way. Imagine a vast *maidan* as flat as a billiard table, with a big grand stand in the centre and enormous stands at the sides—a ground big enough to have a polo match, a game of cricket, and a few football and hockey matches all going on simultaneously. The outer grounds are thronged with soldiers in khaki, soldiers in scarlet, soldiers in dark-green, soldiers in white, British and native, horse, foot, and artillery. Around the grand stand is a throng as gay as at a London church parade; you stumble against Dukes and Lords, jostle Members of Parliament and heads of Administrations, find your path blocked by battalions of military men from every corner of India. The man who conceived the idea of the polo ground and the Polo Club deserves a special honour. He has done more to make the Durbar gathering a social success than probably he himself imagined.

Here you find another world, a retreat wherein Durbars and Investitures become, for the moment at any rate, matters of minor importance. Will Alwar beat Jodhpur? Who will carry off the Hockey Cup? What are the chances for the Football Tournament? These are the subjects discussed, as though the fate of the Empire depended upon the results. And you begin to understand the enthusiasm. Here you see the finest polo in the world, the best football, cricket, and hockey in India. The polo comes first. Morning and afternoon the crowd assembles to watch the splendid play, the magnificently trained ponies, the daring riding, the superb backhand strokes when you think the sweep of the stick will knock the pony off its legs, but instead it sends the ball flying far down the field. The fascination of the game grows upon you; you feel you cannot miss a match. And what fine sportsmen the players are! Did you notice the Patiala back the other day? Sixty-two years of age, but playing with the vigour of twenty-five. Two years ago he retired from the field, but when his team entered for the Durbar Tournament the services of probably the finest back in the world were needed, and he turned out again. In a rush to the line his pony looked like dashing into the spectators, and the fine old player drew it up so sharply that he pulled it clean over backwards on top of him. A damaged shoulder and enforced retirement were the worst of luck, for Patiala lost, and their veteran back has probably played his final game at last. The polo grounds are perfect, absolutely flat, fast, and looked after as carefully as a cricket pitch. "I am going to try and stay on a month after the Durbar," you hear a young officer say, "simply to play polo on these grounds; they are truly marvellous."

Stroll across to the other side. There is Tommy Atkins in strong force watching a football match. Association is the soldier's game. Coming from the Amphitheatre the other day I saw upon an open space, three inches deep in dust, a few soldiers playing football. Every kick sent up a cloud, and the game was going on in an atmosphere so thick that you could hardly see the ball. But Tommy gave an occasional kick at the ball, and was perfectly happy. This is the spirit which draws hundreds of men from the huge army to the polo grounds every day in the hope of seeing a Cup match. The native troops are equally keen on hockey, and play it remarkably well, for they are wonderfully quick and shoot hard and straight.

But sport is not the only attraction. Here play the massed bands, led by Captain Sanford, with the precision and unison of a famous orchestra. You realise the difficulty of conducting a band of two thousand instruments. The most difficult pieces are given, and expert musicians are loud in their praise of the control Captain Sanford has gained over his men. I hear to-day that he will produce before the Viceregal party one afternoon this week the fanfare specially composed by Professor Sir Charles Villiers Stanford, somewhat similar to the long fanfares first performed at state ceremonies in Germany, and now revived by the Kaiser after the discovery at Potsdam of some of the old music written for the Trumpeters of the Guard. The intricate score comprises twelve separate trumpet parts, with an accompaniment of drums and symbals, and the experiment will be an interesting event in the musical world.

These attractions, and the fact that it is the chief social resort in the Durbar camps, fills the polo ground twice daily. And on an off day, just as to-day, the throng is thicker than ever, and you are able to realise the remarkable character of the multitude encamped around the Imperial City. Here are representatives of the Administration, the native princes, the army, and the people. It is India in miniature.

L. E. N.

XVI.

THE PROPHECY.

January 6.

TWO hundred and twenty-seven years ago a Guru, an apostle of the Sikhs, was in captivity in a small building in the Chandni Chauk, at Delhi. He was Teg Bahadur, the ninth in succession of the great Gurus who welded the Sikhs into a band of Asiatic Ironsides, inspired by pure religious zeal, made valiant by the most rigorous military discipline. Teg Bahadur had fallen into the clutches of the great Emperor Aurangzeb, who was eager to compass his doom. At last a false charge was trumped up against him. He was accused of having, when outside his prison, stared curiously in the direction of the Great Mogul's zenana. Questioned as to his alleged crime he answered proudly: "I was not looking towards the zenana. I was looking south for the White Race coming from beyond the sea to tear down thy purdahs and destroy thine empire." The words sealed his doom. He was taken back to his dungeon and beheaded by the order of the incensed potentate. But his words lived in the memory of the persecuted Sikhs. His prophecy was spread far and wide by Govind Singh, the tenth and the greatest Guru, who finally consolidated the Sikhs into a religious and political power destined to become dominant when the Mogul Empire crumbled to pieces. And on the day when John Nicholson led the assault on Delhi, which ended the Mogul reign for ever, the Sikh troops who helped to storm the breaches shouted aloud the prophecy of their martyred Guru. To-day was the birthday of Govind Singh, an anniversary held sacred by all Sikhs, when they meet in their temples to offer prayer to his memory. It was decided by the leading Sikh Maharajahs now at the Imperial Assemblage to go in solemn procession to the shrine of Teg Bahadur and do homage to the name of Govind Singh, and renew their vows of loyalty to the King-Emperor upon that venerated spot. For the little prison is now a temple and place of pilgrimage hallowed by the people for whose sake the saintly Guru died. The ceremony was only witnessed by about a dozen Europeans, for it had not been publicly announced. But thousands of Sikhs from all over Northern India were there, drawn together by a common motive. It was one of the most dramatic events of this eventful gathering. For this Durbar marks the final fulfilment of the prophecy. Here in Imperial Delhi the monarch of the "White Race from beyond the sea" has just proclaimed his right to rule over a vaster Empire than the Moguls ever knew. By the aid of the gallant Sikhs the prediction has been justified to the letter. And it was a sight worth seeing, that of the Sikhs flocking to do homage to the King-

Emperor upon the very spot where their leader laid down his life for his faith. It was something that a patriotic Englishman, remembering how completely the vision of the Guru had been realised, could not contemplate without a thrill of pride.

The building is cramped and narrow and opens on to the Chauk through a narrow archway. Naturally we could not enter the dim shrine within, which was crowded with worshippers. The little courtyard was thronged with Sikhs, some wearing the King's uniform, others those of native chiefs. Men were seated on the ground playing tom-toms. One was stolidly grinding out monotonous music from a miniature harmonium. All wore, either inside or outside their turbans, the thin iron circlet of the Sikhs, which in olden days served both as a protection for the head and as a weapon of offence. The ancient Sikhs could hurl it with marvellous accuracy, and even in modern times it might be made an ugly missile. The roofs of the surrounding buildings were swarming with Sikh women gorgeously attired. Without, a crowd of Sikhs blocked the roadway, though some amount of order was kept by a regiment of Patiala Infantry in their scarlet uniforms. While we were waiting an interesting incident occurred. Ambling along beneath the leafy trees came a remarkable figure astride a tiny pony. It was an old, old man with long white hair, a thin white beard, a haggard face and gleaming eyes. Upon his head he wore an enormous conical structure surrounded by several of the sharp iron circlets and other weapons. His body was clad in a coat of chain mail, and heavy breast-plates protected him in front and back. Slung behind him was a quaint bow and a sheaf of arrows. In his right hand he carried a spear. His feet were bound in blue cloth, but his legs and thighs were bare. He was one of the now dwindling sect of Akalis, the fanatical devotees who carried the tenets of Sikhism to their extreme limit, and in olden times fought and died for them with joyful readiness. The Akalis were once the Ghazis of the Sikh race, the most strenuous professors of the new religion. The aged warrior approached the shrine in triumph. He checked his pony before the lines of troops. They greeted him with a ringing cheer, such a cheer as was not heard in the streets of Delhi even on the day of the State Entry. Waving his spear he chanted in a high resounding voice the names of the Ten Gurus. Then he recited a prayer, and continued with an exhortation, reminding the Sikhs of the valour and the greatness of their race, and urging them never to forget the teachings of their Holy Book or to fail in their loyalty to the British. Finally, he shouted aloud one of the national cries, "Sat Sri Akal," which a Sikh bystander afterwards translated to me thus : "Only the Timeless One is real." The effect was magical. The lines of soldiers shouted aloud the cry, and the crowd took it up far along the Chauk.

Strains of music were heard approaching. The Maharajahs were in sight. A long glittering procession was advancing beneath the trees. First came some mounted drummers and trumpeters, then a squadron of the blue-clad Patiala Lancers. After them came syces leading a string of splendid Arab horses richly caparisoned in bright velvets, then followed a mounted band, and after that a man on horseback carrying a vast curved war horn made of embossed gold hung with golden fringes. Then, strangest feature of all, a handsome carriage. On its back seat in the place of honour lay a great silken quilt covering the Granth, the Sacred Book of the Sikhs. On the front seat sat an attendant splendidly attired, holding a long *chowrie* which he reverently waved over the volume. There was a hush as the carriage halted before the entrance to the shrine. Then the great horn sounded and the bands—there were two of them, one with brass instruments and one with bagpipes—burst forth into "God save the King." It was a curious salutation for the Sikh Scriptures, but somehow, remembering their history, it sounded eminently appropriate.

After the Granth had been solemnly carried into the shrine the procession moved onwards. Next came into view the great gold and silver State carriage of the Patiala Maharajahs, the most wonderful vehicle I have yet seen in this city of strange sights. It was drawn by four horses with outriders in green and gold. Within it was seated the boy Maharajah, who looked as dignified and composed as the oldest of his nobles. He was clad in a golden robe, and the three dignitaries who rode with him were magnificently arrayed in ivory satin, pale green, and light pink, respectively. Footmen carrying silver spears and maces walked around his carriage. He was cheered again and again. As he alighted and entered the shrine—O weird incongruity!—the bagpipes struck up the familiar air of "The Campbells are Coming." For this observance was a purely unofficial function arranged by the Maharajahs themselves, governed by no programme, bound by no restrictions. The aged Maharajah of Nabha, a venerable but impressive potentate, and the Maharajahs of Jind, Kalsia, Faridkote, and Kapurthala followed, each with his escort, his footmen and chobdars, his noisy band and his showy equipage. One by one they entered the shrine and joined together in prayer, and renewed their vows to their new Emperor upon the spot where Teg Bahadur was slain for testifying to the truth as he conceived it. When you thought of the martyred ascetic, of his vision of the White Race from over the ocean, of the gallant Sikhs fighting for Great Britain in the streets of Delhi, and, last and strangest scene of all, of the Sikhs themselves saluting their sacred book that morning with the British National Anthem, you felt that here was a moving picture which, could they but see it, might well give pause to the enemies of England.

XVII.

PRINCES OF INDIA.

January 6.

TO the visitors from Europe nothing in the Durbar ceremonies has been more interesting than the appearance of the ruling chiefs. Their splendid costumes, their clusters of gems, and their quaint retainers have been a continual delight. The variety of the assemblages has brought home more than any figures can do the vastness of the Indian Empire. One realises at last the real meaning of the fact that the Indian princes hold sway over 655,000 square miles of territory, with a population exceeding 63 millions—a people more numerous by fourteen millions than the inhabitants of the German Empire. There are to-day a hundred and twelve chiefs encamped around Delhi.

The ruler whose movements have attracted the greatest attention is naturally his Highness the Nizam, whose state contains over eleven millions of people, and whose revenue is forty millions of rupees a year. Although personally adhering to marked simplicity in dress, his temporary residence at Ludlow Castle, rented from the Delhi Club, is furnished in magnificent style. The private apartments contain the most costly carpets, hangings and shawls, many of them the work of

Kishen Chand, the famous shawl merchant who made some of the Coronation robes for Queen Alexandra; and at the garden party he gave a few days ago there was an unparalleled display of gold plate. The grounds of the Castle are gaily decorated, yellow, the royal colour at Hyderabad, predominating, whilst his carriage and escort of regal splendour has been one of the sights of Delhi.

Far away on the other side of the camps is the residence of the Gaekwar of Baroda. The bungalow was built in Baroda. It is a substantial structure with glass windows and doors, and at the side is a beautifully furnished durbar tent. At the back one catches a glimpse of the big engines which work the electric light installation and the water pumps. The arrangements and decorations of the camp are perfect, and the pretty illuminations at night attract large crowds of natives. The famous guns are objects of interest to every passer by. One is made of solid gold and is mounted on a carriage of silver; the other is of silver upon a gilded carriage. They are drawn by oxen with gold trappings, with pure gold sheaths on their horns, and heavy gold anklets on their legs. Perhaps the most striking feature of the Gaekwar's camp is the magnificent display of jewels. At the Durbar his Highness wore a breast-plate of diamonds worth nearly a quarter of a million sterling. The private apartments are a storehouse of jewels, which are guarded by armed men. One pearl necklace of extraordinary beauty is valued at 36 lakhs of rupees, and is one of the finest in the world.

Although unmarked by any great display of wealth, the camps of the great Rajput chiefs are well worth a visit. The retainers of the Maharajah of Jaipur number 1,197, and three special trains were needed to bring them to Delhi, though the animals, including five elephants and one hundred and fifty horses and camels, marched by road all the way from Jaipur. The Jaipur Imperial Service Corps of a thousand ponies and five hundred carts took a prominent part in the great manœuvres which preceded the Durbar. The kanats which surround the camp are supported by iron rails, originally utilized for the purpose of a tramway to convey all the baggage of the Maharajah from the station to the camp. The charming Udaipur camp was laid out under the personal direction of the Maharana. Two special trains brought the thousand retainers and servants to Delhi, and three magnificent elephants came by road. It has been a matter for general regret that illness prevented his Highness taking part in the State Entry and Durbar. A handsome arch marks the entrance to the Bikanir camp of two hundred tents. Five elephants were brought, and a collection of jewels which has dazzled the eyes of those privileged to see it.

The young ruler of Mysore has his camp near to that of the Gaekwar. There are steel and plaster residences for the Maharajah and the Dewan, mess houses for the European and native guests, and a great durbar tent; the camp is lighted by electricity. Six special trains were required to bring the Maharajah's Imperial Service Lancers, followers, horses, carriages and retainers to Delhi. Mysore has long been famous for its elephants, and the one his Highness rode at the State Entry was a truly royal animal. The Maharajah wore on that occasion a dress of gold brocade, with magnificent diamonds, strings of pearls and a pendant of rubies. Among the most popular princes here is Scindia, who has been an invariable attendant at all the big functions. His camp is laid out in a semicircle, and is lighted by gas. The Maharajah is accompanied by the British Resident, the Dowager-Maharani, the Maharani Scindia, nine Sardars, four European officers, and fifteen hundred retainers, including detachments from various irregular corps maintained by the State. No fewer than eighteen elephants were brought. His Highness's costumes have been much admired. At the State Entry he wore a dark red silk coat, richly embroidered, and the Scindia turban, his jewellery consisting of fine diamonds; at the Durbar his pink embroidered coat was covered with jewels; and at the Investiture his costume was of light yellow adorned with emeralds. The Kashmir camp occupies an area of two hundred yards by five hundred yards, fenced off from the road by neat bamboo railings. The centre road leads through a well-laid lawn to the durbar tent, which is supported by silver poles with gold balls at the top. The lining of the tent is embroidered in exquisite Kashmir needlework, whilst the carpets are of the finest Kashmir work. The camp contains four hundred tents and is lighted by electricity, and the visitors include the Mirs of Hunza and Nagar, the Raja of Poonah, and other frontier chiefs feudatory to Kashmir. At the Durbar his Highness and his brother appeared in splendid yet simple costumes, with the beautiful plume which is the emblem of the Dogra Raj waving from their turbans, while the jewellery of the young Prince Hari Singh, son of Raja Sir Amar Singh, included a superb necklace of pearls.

The brightness of the Punjab camps is a pleasing change from the dusty areas nearer Delhi. The tents are gay with flags ; strings of bunting and lines of coloured fairy lamps look pretty in the morning sunshine. Here you find the Nawab of Bahawalpur, the Nawab of Dujana, the Raja of Faridkot, the Raja of Jind, the Sardar of Kalsia, the Raja of Kapurthala, the Raja of Keonthal, the Nawab of Loharu, the son of the Nawab of Maler Kotla, the Raja of Nabha, the Raja of Nalagarh, the young Maharajah of Patiala and the Raja of Sirmur. The street is full of India's fighting men. Pathans jostle Sikhs and Beluchis at every corner. A Patiala syce leads forward a pretty white-grey pony with elaborately embroidered gold trappings. It is the property of the boy ruler, who, although only eleven years of age, will ride it at the head of his troops at the great review. Then comes a splendid elephant with a howdah of gold and silver and a jhool so richly embroidered as to defy description; servants in scarlet carrying fans of gold; men bearing two mighty umbrellas; marvellous gold and silver palkies. All these treasures are freely brought out and an enormous amount of time taken in arranging a private view to please a few visitors. Then you can see the greyhounds in red coats, and the hawks—carried by brightly uniformed servants—of the sporting Raja of Nabha.

In the absence of the Maharajah of Sikkim, through illness, his son and heir, Sikhyong Tulka, has represented him, the party including Dewan Jerong, the Kaziz of Yangthang and Barmiak, Rinzing Kazi of Ringen, the well known explorer, and some sixty retainers, whilst Ujen Kazi, the vakil of the independent state of Bhutan, is a guest. The camp is one of the most interesting places at Delhi. One side is wholly Thibetan in design and material. A row of tall masts with prayers printed on red, green and blue cloth, leads to the entrance to a large courtyard formed of Thibetan cloth emblazoned with emblems of good luck, the interlaced circles being conspicuous. The centre of the courtyard is occupied by the same sign worked in flowering plants, and the walls are adorned with ancient portraits of saints painted on large banners. The roof of the main room is covered with signs, the head and hands of the protecting demon being conspicuous, while the eight emblems of happiness are worked in colours, four on the front of the tent and four at the back. The interior displays a complete Lama altar with impressive specimens of ecclesiastical work in gold and silver plate; on the walls are ancient emblems of embroidered priestly robes, surmounted by unique aprons of carved human bones. Scattered about are quaint swords, handsome rings, enormous trumpets, and various curios from Thibet. This is the first occasion on which a complete Thibetan camp has been seen in the plains of India.

But the most picturesque figures in the Durbar camp are the men from the Shan State. The chiefs appear in the old court dress of the time of the Kings of Burma. The strange high headdresses of gold, and the robes with gold wings, after the fashion of Buddhist dewas or saints, are very curious. The costume is heavy, and the old Sawbwa of Mong Nai, who rode his elephant in the procession, was quite exhausted at the close of the day. The premier Shan Chief is the Sawbwa of Keng Tung, whose state borders on China, Siam, and French territory. He and his sister Top Htila rode together in the State procession. To reach Delhi they started in November and rode five hundred miles to the rail head. The second chief is the Sawbwa of Mong Nai, premier chief west of the Salween, whose courtly manner has made him a general favourite. Amongst those in carriages were Yawnghwe and his Mahadevi, the only lady with a title from the Burmese Court; Touth

Hsenwi from the Northern States, who has fifty wives and goes by the title of The Flower Round Whom the Butterflies Flutter; Mong Pawn, noted for his zeal in public works and for never finishing a sentence; Kantarawadi, the chief of the Red Karens, plainly dressed, with a face as unmoved as if it was carved in oak; and Hauguiongham, the representative of the tribes in the debatable land between Burma and the Shan Hills. Many of them have never seen the sea before, none of them have ever been in India; and it says much for their self-control that they regarded the gorgeous retinues of the Indian princes and the strength of the great Army without visible signs of astonishment.

The Raja of Kapurthala brought an elephant with a howdah especially made for the Durbar, and his Highness and his eleven-year old son wore handsome costumes. The former had a splendid tiara of costly gems, and rode in a coach imported from Europe for the occasion, escorted by a fine body of men in smart blue and white uniforms. The Maharajah of Cooch Behar displayed gorgeous dresses and jewels, and the costumes of the Maharajah of Benares were noticeable even in the blaze of colour at the Amphitheatre, his dress being of gold covered with pearls, brilliants and rubies. In the camps of the Bengal chiefs, the durbar tent of the Maharajah Bahadur of Durbhanga is conspicuous for its silver pillars and costly carpets. His Highness's Durbar dress was superb. The head dress was the orthodox Mithila puggaree, adorned with a diamond aigrette with an immense diamond in the centre; he wore a pearl and diamond necklace of great value; and his coat and overcoat were of the richest velvet embroidered with gold.

These are only a few of the representative Indian chiefs assembled at Delhi. But incomplete as the list necessarily is, it will give some idea of the magnificent spectacles associated with the historic event of January 1st.

L. E. N.

XVIII.

THE STATE BALL.

January 7.

IT is curious and rather amusing to reflect how many predictions about this Imperial Assemblage have been falsified. For instance, it was said that plague would turn the camp into a vast charnel house. It was said that there would be innumerable deaths from pneumonia among visitors unaccustomed to the rigours of tent life in the Punjab. It was said that fires would sweep away acres of tents. It was said that the elephants would never march in procession through Delhi, and that the first one that met a motor-car would run amok. It was said that the Durbar would be a hopeless muddle and a failure. It was said that none of the preparations for any single function would be completed in time. It was said that heavy rainfall would inevitably ruin the principal spectacles and turn the camp into one huge swamp. It was said, though no one seemed quite ready to explain why, that the Viceroy would destroy his great reputation and wreck his career in consequence of the certain ignominious breakdown of the whole project. None of these things have happened. In every respect the prescience of the Viceroy and the ability of his chosen assistants have been signally vindicated. Every gathering has been a triumphant success, everything that was planned has been carried out precisely as was ordained. But in no single instance have the prognostications of the prophets of evil been more remarkably falsified than in the case of the State Ball held last night in the Diwan-i-Am and the Diwan-i-Khas. For though dismal forebodings have abounded about every event, they found their fine flower in gloomy assertions about the fate of the State Ball. You met men with mathematical minds who had made fearsome calculations about the time it would take to deposit the guests at the gates of the Fort. They were ready to prove to you that supposing each carriage disgorged its occupants with the utmost rapidity, it would take until ten o'clock next morning for all those invited to enter the Diwan-i-Am. There were others who professed to have worked out the relative capacities of the Black Hole of Calcutta and the Diwan-i-Am, taking into account the estimated difference in the number of occupants. They were eager to show you that the horrors of the Black Hole were destined to be reproduced on an intensified scale. Nearly everybody was convinced that there would be no dancing. A rumour that the Viceroy insisted upon having a set of State Lancers was smiled at with pitying sorrow for his Excellency's folly. Few people expected to get any supper. Fewer still expected to find their carriages after everything was over. Yet everyone was bent on going, not because they hoped for enjoyment, but because they wanted to say afterwards that they were there.

It all showed the uncertainty of human anticipations. Not only did everybody go—that is, everybody who received an invitation—but all who were there enjoyed themselves hugely. None of the dismal vaticinations were realised. There was never at any time lack of elbow room. The State Lancers were duly danced without difficulty. The floor, though not ideal, was as reasonably good as could have been expected. There was plenty of space for dancing before midnight, and any quantity of room afterwards. The cloak-room arrangements were perfect, and everybody got their cloaks and wraps promptly when they wanted them. There was no jam of carriages, largely owing to the fact that many people elected to travel on the light railway from the Central Camp to the Selimgarh entrance to the Fort, whence a covered way of inordinate length led to the very doors of the Diwan-i-Am. It was always possible to obtain refreshments at the buffets in the corners of the ball-room at any moment. The supply of drinks and ices and light eatables seemed inexhaustible. The expected famine did not supervene. An excellent supper was served in the Diwan-i-Khas, where the wants of all were ministered to in swift abundance. It certainly took a little time to reach the supper-room during the earlier hours, but who would not mind waiting a few minutes to sup in the jewelled marble halls of Shah Jehan? The whole gathering was a magnificent success and a triumph of organisation. There was no hitch from start to finish. Nothing untoward occurred, and dancing was kept up until nearly four in the morning. And as for the supposed difficulty of reaching the scene of the Ball, I can only say that by half-past nine nearly all the guests had arrived and were waiting the advent of the Viceroy and the Royalties.

To get the best conception of the brilliance of the scene you had to climb to one of the band galleries at either end of the hall. It was truly a wonderful sight. The great building with massive red arches was filled with the most resplendent throng it has ever been my fortune to gaze upon. Uniforms were overpoweringly preponderant. Every regiment in the Army seemed to be represented. All the political and civil officials were also in full uniform. But these were features that one can often see. What made the splendour and the novelty of the occasion were the magnificent costumes of the ruling chiefs and their relatives, who appeared to have been reserving their most gorgeous apparel for this event. They were attired in the richest silks and satins of striking hues, and many of them were blazing with jewels. The same may be said of the English ladies, and probably no such array of handsome dresses has ever been seen in India before. Feminine dress has certainly been one of the most notable features of this Assemblage, even to the undiscerning and unimpressionable male spectator. But neither the Durbar nor the Investiture could compare in point of dress with last night's Ball. Every lady was in her newest and most fascinating toilet. It was evident that to the ladies now in Delhi the Ball was the principal event of the whole ten days. And the display of jewels was equally unparalleled. Never has such an array of diamonds been seen—there must have been as many diamonds as all the fabled stores of Golconda ever produced. But I will not dilate in detail upon the grandeur of the spectacle. A famous journalist was heard to say to-day that he had used his last adjective. That expresses my own feeling. Yet I wish that another pen, not wearied of the impossible task of adequately framing in words the picture of these days at Delhi, could describe for you that mighty hall full of bright light, and the throng that ceaselessly moved about it. No one seems to know precisely how many were there, but the guests cannot have numbered far short of five thousand. They filled its every part, but were thickest around the space before the great white marble recess and canopy where Shah Jehan used to sit in audience.

Shortly after ten o'clock the strains of the National Anthem announced the arrival of the Viceroy and Lady Curzon, the Duke and Duchess of Connaught, the Grand Duke of Hesse, and the rest of the notabilities. Their Excellencies and their Royal Highnesses proceeded at once to the dais, whence they surveyed the glittering crowd before them. Then came the opening dance, the State Lancers. The Viceroy, who was wearing the riband of the Star of India, had as his partner the Duchess of Connaught, the Duke of Connaught danced with Lady Curzon, the Grand Duke of Hesse with Lady Northcote, Lord Northcote with Lady Ampthill, Lord Ampthill with the Duchess of Portland, Lord Kitchener with Mrs. Bourdillon, Sir F. Fryer with the Duchess of Marlborough, and Sir Charles Rivaz with Lady La Touche.

The Duchess of Connaught was wearing a white dress, the skirt being trimmed with gold embroidery. Lady Curzon's dress baffles description; it conveyed an impression of shimmering gold shot with peacock blue. It was amusing to listen to the comments of the spectators while the dance was in progress. For once the Viceregal and Royal party was to some extent disregarded. The real centre of interest was Lord Kitchener. Thousands were watching to see how he comported himself in this unwonted relaxation. But his Excellency seemed blissfully unconscious of the attention he was arousing, and went through the dance with a smiling face, and without any discernible mistakes. He may not be a graceful dancer, but at any rate he has mastered the intricacies of the lancers with his usual thoroughness. After the lancers were over dancing began in real earnest, and was continued with the utmost vigour. Meanwhile the Viceroy and the Duke and Duchess had returned to the dais, where they were joined by Lord and Lady Northcote and Lord and Lady Ampthill. The leading princes then in turn ascended the dais to greet them, and some time was spent in conversation. The Nizam, who was dressed in his accustomed plain black, with a yellow headdress, was the first to be presented. Among the other chiefs no one attracted more attention than the handsome Rao of Cutch. To the disappointment of many the Gaekwar of Baroda did not wear his famous diamond necklace, which has as its central stone the Star of the South, one of the biggest diamonds in the world. His Highness contented himself with a smaller chain of diamonds, which were nevertheless of a size and purity which many a millionaire would envy. After a time, the Viceroy and the Duke of Connaught descended from the dais and conversed in turn with many of the chiefs and nobles.

At eleven o'clock the principal guests proceeded to the Diwan-i-Khas to supper. Afterwards the rest of the guests were admitted to the supper-room in batches. The way thither was kept by long lines of troopers of the 4th Dragoon Guards—tall, stalwart men in gleaming helmets with white plumes, carrying their lances and standing stolid and immoveable. Reaching the Diwan-i-Khas was necessarily rather a prolonged business, but the loveliness of the place fully repaid the slight delays that occurred. Contrary to expectation, no tables were actually laid in the Diwan-i-Khas itself. It has been explained in previous letters that two wings have been temporarily added to the Hall of Private Audience, one connecting it with the Royal

Baths, and the other with the Royal Apartments. It was in these two temporary structures that supper was served. The visible effect was that of one long continuous marble hall with supper in progress at either end, but the centre portion quite clear save for a few chairs. The Diwan-i-Khas is beautiful beyond compare in the daytime, but at night, in a blaze of light, it takes unto itself a new and more glorious splendour. Those who looked along the vista of shining marble arches and floors, jewelled and decorated with perfect grace, felt that it was a privilege they would not have lightly missed. It is something to have supped in the midst of that pearly purity of marble.

For the rest, it must suffice to say that the Duke and Duchess of Connaught did not leave the Ball until after midnight. The Viceroy and Lady Curzon stayed some time longer. Many of the most distinguished guests were still dancing merrily long after three. The floor was becoming clear then, and there was room for all and to spare. Some of the guests did not reach the more distant camps until five in the morning. It was a memorable night, and its finest feature was that it was the success which few people anticipated. Small wonder that, as many noticed, the Viceroy looked pleased and happy. For all the things that he conceived have come to pass, the last of the great official functions has been triumphantly concluded, and Asia has witnessed a series of pageants that will live in history for all time.

XIX.

A MOTLEY ARMY.

January 7.

AN artist friend told me how to see the review of chiefs' retinues to-day. He said:—"Don't be satisfied with sitting in that Amphitheatre and seeing them go round like a circus. Get up early, and watch them arrive on the plain outside. That's the place to see things." It was rather a trial to turn out before seven, when the State Ball had kept one from bed until after four; but it was worth it. The plain was covered with a most amazing throng. The very first group that met the gaze was a gang of Arabs armed with ancient muskets, cheek by jowl with a knot of Shans carrying murderous *dahs* and smoking big cheroots. The whole scene was a medley of mediævalism. It was an aspect of India that was a revelation to people who have clung to beaten tracks. Even experienced political officers, familiar with native states, had to admit that many types were strange to them, many costumes absolutely unknown. And I met a man from Bombay who exclaimed:—"I thought I knew India, but feel now as though I had lived in Chicago all my life. This is a new world to me." Perhaps these first impressions were a little too pronounced. After all, even this was not quite the real India. Many of the dresses had only been prepared for the occasion. But it was the India of a century ago, reproduced in living reality; and it derived its impressiveness from the fact that there were retainers there from every state in the Indian Empire. You might, perhaps, on a special occasion, see in a native state just a handful of these strange figures; but such a motley army has never been collected in one place before, and probably never will be again. And as for colour, the State Entry and the Durbar were in monotones compared to this. One master of his art, whose name is familiar in two hemispheres, positively groaned with dismay when he looked upon it. Even his magic palette was not equal to the task.

It is hard to disentangle isolated features from a series of blurred impressions; but the effort must be made. To seek to convey an idea of the spectacle in the mass is hopeless; I can only single out examples at random. Very early in my wanderings through the crowd, I came upon a great coach drawn by elephants, sent by the Maharajah of Rewa. It was painted light blue, with a light brown roof. Its interior was the size of a small drawing room, and was furnished with comfortable arm chairs. The elephants which drew it wore trappings of blue and gold. I was still staring at this ponderous conveyance, when one of the Rewa Sirdars trotted up. He was dressed in a cream-coloured robe richly embroidered with a floral design. His turban was green. In his hand he carried a slender lance, at his waist was slung a great sword with a green velvet scabbard, and at his back was a shield. His horse bore a massive silver headdress, surmounted by a silver peacock. His saddle-cloth was of green velvet with silver bosses; all his saddlery was enriched with silver. You fancied he was an unique apparition until you discovered half-a-dozen more like him, wandering about hard by. And then you came upon the Rewa irregular troops, the cavalry in green with yellow facings and turban, the infantry in an aggressive blue that startled your still sleepy eyes. After these revelations, you contemplated Rewa's great silver palanquin, fashioned like a lion, with comparative equanimity.

Close at hand stood Holkar's elephants, one with a vast golden howdah upholstered in green velvet. The very tail straps were covered with golden bosses, and the vast jhool was of crimson velvet embroidered with gold. Beside them stood the Maharajah's famous Arabs, held by syces in yellow and bright blue, with suns emblazoned on the breast of their tunics. One of these horses, a pure white, is reputed to be the finest Arab in India. The gold and silver guns of the Gaekwar of Baroda have been written about before; but not, perhaps, the stalwart shikaris of the Maharajah of Mysore, clad in scarlet, and carrying spears tied up with bunches of green muslin. Nor have readers learned, perchance, of the followers of that Arabian potentate, the Sultan of Shehr and Makalla, tattered cavalry and infantry in scarlet with yellow facings and the hooded headgear of the desert, carrying old muskets, rusty shields, and quaint tomtoms. The Mir of

Khairpur affected quieter colours, for his troops were in rifle green tunics with red facings, and baggy brown breeches ; but the howdah on his elephant was covered by a canopy in rainbow hues.

The Rao of Cutch contributed to the gathering a faithful reproduction of a procession held in his state a hundred years ago, and duly recorded in panoramic pictures by native artists of the period. To recite all its features would necessitate a separate article; but you noticed camel-men in red with violet turbans ; standard bearers carrying banners surmounted by gilded heads of elephants and dragons ; soldiers completely enveloped in chain armour, and mounted on ponies ; other warriors protected by breast plates ; and men in scarlet with immense silver trumpets. The Shans from the remotest confines of Burma, clad in green velvet jackets and loose mauve velvet trousers, each with his ivory-handled *dah* and his vast straw hat,—many with gilt umbrellas,—were a general object of interest. The Bhopal irregular cavalry looked very smart in their coats and turbans of chocolate and gold, and their white breeches ; but the feature of the Bhopal display was the elephants bearing men in chain armour, with spiked helmets surmounted by plumes of green feathers. The Orcha cavalry were plainly attired in khaki with blue turbans ; the unmounted irregulars were gaudy in green and lemon-yellow.

But the spectacle which made every Englishman who saw it catch his breath with astonishment, was the sight of some cavalry sent by the Maharajah of Jaipur. Fancy coming suddenly, unexpectedly, without the slightest warning, upon a whole squadron of horsemen in chain armour, standing silent and grim and impassive! It was like a page out of Scott, like meeting the friends and foes of boyhood. On every casque there nodded a tossing golden plume, on every lance in rest there fluttered a red and white pennon. You were struck at once by the sinister and forbidding aspect of these taciturn mail-clad lancers. A host of armoured horsemen must have looked far more stern and formidable, to outward seeming, than a modern cavalry division in khaki. Our ironclads are infinitely more awe-inspiring than the warships of the Middle Ages; a reverse process seems to have been at work among the land forces. The Datia State had carried the idea of armour still farther, for it had even an elephant clad in a coat of mail. Datia also sent a contingent of mail-clad warriors, who had pink tunics beneath their open-work armour, very much as a lady wears pink under light muslin. Their steel caps were bound with bright scarves, in their hands they carried spears, and at their backs were slung—bows and arrows! From Dhar came elephants manned by fierce warriors with blue-black beards, clad in crimson velvet. The elephants were surrounded by foot guards armed with bell-mouthed blunderbusses, and preceded by retainers in maroon and yellow. Charkhari sent men in scarlet on camels, lancers in vivid green with yellow facings and blue puggarees, and a mob of footmen in crimson lake trimmed with green.

The recital of colours may be tedious, but in no other way can the blazing hues of the crowds swarming on the plain be conveyed. Jodhpur's irregular infantry were a little more subdued, in dark green with red trousers; but the feature of the Jodhpur display was the now inevitable mail-clad cavalry, with heavy visored helmets, mounted on some of the splendid horses for which the state is famous. It was reserved to Bikanir to introduce a novel effect in the matter of mailed men, a feature outside the ken of Western tales of chivalry. The desert state had mounted fifty sheathed warriors on camels, each with a chrome yellow and rice green saddle cloth. They passed in procession quite noiselessly, the only audible sound being the gentle pad-pad of the camels, and the slight rustling of the loose flexible armour. The camelry were followed by a throng of mounted retainers with silver-adorned saddlery; every man carried at his back a polished shield of hippopotamus hide. From Kotah came horsemen in orange yellow, swarms of footmen in light blue and red, and some nearly naked ascetics with bodies smeared an ashen colour. These last were armed with bucklers and huge swords, and as they afterwards passed around the arena they fought mock duels, to the intense amusement of the spectators. Near these weird fanatics stood a full company of men from Kishengarh, attired in vast robes of slate-blue tint. At the first glance they looked liked cowled monks; then you wondered whether they were nobles in hooded dressing gowns; finally you perceived that they carried swords, and that their dress was a huge quilted coat stuffed with cotton. And excellent garments they must have been, too, for warding off sword-cuts, though rather oppressive to wear in the sandy wastes of Rajputana; doubtless they were the outcome of human ingenuity triumphing over the scarcity and costliness of iron. Their high conical quilted headgear was bound with cords of green and black. Kishengarh also sent a squadron of mailed horsemen, with steel caps like cupolas, crowned by glittering tufts of silver thread, and with steel veils. Four of these redoubtable warriors created a sensation by standing erect on their horses in the procession.

The state of Alwar made a brave show. One of the Alwar elephants had great chandeliers affixed to its tusks; what intensified the grotesque effect was that the glasses were stuffed full of crimson asters! Its jhool was gold-embroidered; its mahout was gorgeous in cloth of gold; the sides of its howdah were fashioned into golden rampant lions. Alwar also had an elephant carriage two stories high, almost big enough to make a respectable cottage. The upper story was covered by a canopy. The feats of horsemanship of some of the Alwar horsemen as they afterwards passed before the Viceroy, aroused the utmost enthusiasm. The Maharajah of Benares sent an extraordinary and variegated throng of followers; his elephants and howdahs were unusually imposing. But to catalogue all the fantastic sights one saw would be an endless task. There were men from the monasteries of far Ladak with huge grinning dragon masks, and a skull and crossbones worked upon their tattered dress of Chinese embroidery; Buddhist abbots from the lamaserais, clad in yellow, with shaven heads; the two famous giants of Kashmir, over eight feet high, with enormous hands and feet; lancers from Jammu with bright brass helmets, and blue tunics covered with breastplates; Patiala's wonderful gold and silver state carriage, upholstered in salmon pink, and drawn by four white horses; Jind's carriage, scarcely less resplendent; the sporting old Maharaja of Nabha's noted greyhounds, horses, and dogs; Faridkot's great waggonette drawn by four camels; the smart irregular infantry of Kolhapur; the Cutch fighting men on stilts—not purposeless, as some supposed, but meant to attack warriors in howdahs; a splendid procession of fifteen massive elephants from Gwalior; Holkar's cavalry in Reckitt's blue uniforms, infantry in mustard-colour attire, imposing elephants, and a gorgeous palanquin shaped like a peacock. The subsequent procession around the arena of the Amphitheatre was witnessed by the Viceroy and the Duke and Duchess of Connaught, and a tremendous crowd of spectators. But the eyes were blinded by the colour, the pen revolts from the task of describing it.

XX.

A BIG REVIEW.

January 8.

IT was fitting that the last of the great events in connection with the Durbar should be a grand military review. The Army has been very much in evidence at the various ceremonial gatherings which have been the distinguishing features of this Imperial Assemblage. At every formal function the troops have played a prominent part. Military uniforms have generally predominated everywhere. Delhi has been the centre of a concentration of troops the like of which the city has never witnessed since the British Raj was proclaimed. Yet the great display to-day was not entirely intended as a manifestation of the armed strength which stands behind the just and enlightened rule of India by the British. Rather was it meant to show to the world the inspiring spectacle of thousands and thousands of the fighting races of India cheerfully and voluntarily wearing the King-Emperor's uniform, marshalling themselves beneath his colours, and parading with the British troops whom they have so often fought beside shoulder to shoulder against a common foe. The Native Army of India has proved its loyalty to the Throne on many a battlefield, and it was never in a more efficient condition than now.

An entire Army Corps was on parade this morning at an early hour on the vast level plain which lies almost due west of the Amphitheatre. Close upon thirty thousand troops were under arms. The cavalry alone reached a total of six thousand, and there were very nearly twenty thousand infantry. The force was drawn up in one long line faciug the saluting point, and about a third of a mile distant. It extended almost as far as the eye could see on the right hand and on the left. The flower of the Army in India was assembled in serried array in review order, and as the Army Corps awaited the arrival of the Viceroy you could see flashes, like summer lightning, playing up and down the illimitable lines of bayonets and lances. Before the troops, and exactly opposite the flagstaff, was Lord Kitchener, mounted on a splendid charger, and behind him a large and brilliant staff. At the saluting base were two great stands crammed with spectators, while the edges of the review ground were covered by large throngs of natives. Punctually at half-past ten the guns of a battery roared out a Royal Salute of 31 guns. Lord Curzon had arrived, and was approaching the saluting point. His procession was led by a squadron of the Viceregal Bodyguard, followed by the Imperial Cadets in full uniform and commanded by the Maharajah of Idar. His Excellency, who was mounted on a fine horse, was in morning dress, with a plain white helmet. A single order was fastened to his black frock-coat. He was accompanied by H.R.H. the

Duke of Connaught, who wore the full uniform of a Field Marshal and carried a bâton, and by the Grand Duke of Hesse in a blue uniform. The remainder of the Viceregal Bodyguard concluded the procession. As his Excellency reached the saluting point, Lord Kitchener signalled to the troops the order for a Royal Salute, the massed cavalry band played the National Anthem, and the Royal Standard was unfurled. Meanwhile, the Duchess of Connaught and Lady Curzon had been driven into the central enclosure, whence they witnessed the procession from their carriage. The march past was immediately begun. The whole of the Cavalry Division executed a long wheeling movement to the westward, riding around a half circle in order to get into position for the saluting point. When they were all in motion and about half a mile away they were absolutely concealed by dense clouds of dust. It was curious to witness this sudden and dramatic invisibility of six thousand horsemen. You knew where they were moving, yet could see nothing but a huge cloud of dust; and before the great veil appeared the figure of a solitary galloper racing with an order. The sunlight flashed for a moment upon his accoutrements. Then he plunged through the curtain and was lost to view. Yet somehow, with this single exception, the dust interfered but little with the success of the Review. For the space of a quarter of a mile on each side of the saluting point the whole of the troops were always visible even when in motion. One could only conclude that the plain had been well watered. The massed bands of the entire Cavalry Division announced the approach of the troops. First came Lord Kitchener's staff, followed by the heads of the various military departments, who were in turn succeeded by Sir George Wolseley, Sir Bindon Blood, and Sir Robert Low. Then, riding quite alone and followed by a single orderly, the Commander-in-Chief himself. His Excellency, long sword in hand, saluted slowly and ceremoniously as he passed the saluting point. Then wheeling to the right, he trotted up to the Viceroy, saluted again, and handed in the parade state of the forces. For the remainder of the review he stayed at this point.

The place of honour was occupied by three splendid batteries of Royal Horse Artillery, which went by with admirable alignment. Then followed the First Cavalry Brigade, consisting of the 4th Dragoon Guards, the 15th Hussars, the 4th Bombay Cavalry, and the 9th Bengal Lancers. The 2nd Cavalry Brigade, led by the 9th Lancers, came next. You could hear the crowd cheering the 9th Lancers long before they reached the saluting point. As they passed the grand stand there was a roar of cheers. The fine composite regiment of the Central India Horse kept a splendid line and presented a notably smart appearance. The 4th Brigade consisted of Imperial Service Cavalry, led by that keen soldier, Colonel Stuart Beatson. The regiments, to avoid misunderstandings about precedence, filed past in alphabetical order. The Alwar Lancers, led by their young Chief, one of the finest horsemen in India, came first. But the corps that pleased the onlookers most was the still unblooded Hyderabad Lancers, whose ranks were filled with as good a type of cavalry soldier as India can produce. They went by with the utmost steadiness and precision, every horse in his place to an inch. Cheer after cheer went up when the Patiala Lancers, big bearded men, who sat their horses with surprising lissomeness, marched past. For at their head rode the little eleven-year-old Maharajah of Patiala on a white pony, clad in a turban of the palest green and a robe of cream tinged with salmon pink. His Highness bore himself with great gravity and surprising dignity, and saluted the Viceroy with his little sword with all the composure of the oldest of his warriors. After the Imperial Service Cavalry had passed there came a number of Brigade Divisions of Field, Mountain and Garrison Artillery. All were good, but the pick of the lot was the First Brigade Division of the Royal Field Artillery, consisting of the 13th, 67th, and 69th Batteries, commanded by Colonel Rainsford. Nothing could excel the way in which this Division went past with mathematical precision. Yet they were not parade ground soldiers, for these three batteries have the proud distinction of having fought right through the war in South Africa ; and the men had the marks of hard service still plain in their keen alert faces. They were loudly applauded as they passed, as were also the British Brigade

Division of Mountain Batteries under Major Fagan. The latter are manned by picked men, and they looked it. Two batteries of thirty-pounders, the only two of that arm in India, also came in for much admiration. Followed the Sappers and Miners, the pontoons and balloons, the mounted Volunteers, among whom the blue uniforms of the Bombay Light Horse were readily distinguishable, and the Mounted Infantry. This portion of the march past was ended by a section of the Bikanir Camel Corps, led by the soldierly young Maharajah of Bikanir, in a magnificent uniform.

It is, I fear, impossible to refer in great detail to the march past of the twenty thousand Infantry. I can only allude to a few of the regiments which took part in it. If complete precision, a line not deviating by a hair's breadth, ranks filled by smart well-set-up men, the whole regiment moving like a well-oiled machine, constitute criteria, then the pride of place must be allotted to the 2nd Battalion King's Royal Rifle Corps commanded by Colonel Gore-Brown. The spectators were evidently of the same opinion, for no infantry battalion received a greater ovation. Next to this, popular approval rightly favoured the 1st Battalion of that famous regiment, the Royal Irish Rifles, which headed the brigade commanded by Sir James Willcocks. Another battalion in General Willcocks' brigade that received quite an ovation was the 1st Battalion of the 3rd Gurkhas. It was curious and significant to note how popular all the Gurkha regiments were with the onlookers. Yet another battalion in the 3rd Brigade which aroused loud cheers was the 6th Jats, who swung by in admirable alignment with a light firm tread. On the whole, the 3rd Brigade was the best of the Infantry Brigades, taken as a whole, if the applause of the crowd counts for anything in such matters. Other regiments which made a specially good impression were the 2nd Battalion Welsh Regiment, the 2nd Battalion Argyll and Sutherland Highlanders, the gallant 15th Sikhs, and the 1st Battalion Bedford Regiment, while mention must be made of the 28th Madras Infantry, composed of men of fine physique who went by in excellent style. It would take too long to refer to the Imperial Service Infantry, though I must not forget to record how the venerable and intensely loyal Maharajah of Nabha went by at the head of his Infantry, and how enthusiastic cheers were raised as he trotted back to the saluting point and received the congratulations of the Viceroy and the Duke of Connaught. Nor can I describe at length how, when the Infantry had withdrawn, the Cavalry and Artillery formed up a third of a mile away and advanced at a hand gallop towards the saluting point in three separate divisions; nor how finally the whole great mass of men and guns and horses formed up afresh and galloped over the plain towards us, one great irresistible force which it seemed that nothing could check. It was a fine sight and a fitting close to the greatest and most successful review ever seen in India.

XXI.

AFTERTHOUGHTS.

January 13.

ONE needed a rest after the close of this Imperial Assemblage before attempting to record a few final reflections upon it. Things had temporarily lost their true perspective. The mind had become blurred by so many splendid spectacles unveiled in rapid succession. It was as though a cinematograph had been at work upon a novel principle, revealing not one continuous picture, but a whirling variety of scenes, wherein only the central figures remained the same. For a whole year India had been preparing for the great event. For months beforehand people talked of little else. As the appointed days drew near the tension grew to straining point. Then, suddenly, "Click, click, click!" Almost before you realised it, the machine was in motion, the panorama was being unfolded before your eyes. There was one sharp, quick rush of dazzling scenes, and then it was over, leaving you breathless, astonished, exhausted. "I have been bludgeoned with impressions," said one newspaper man as he sank back into an easy chair after three weeks of the hardest work he had ever known in a busy life. I think that expressed the feeling of most of those who have been in Delhi during this memorable time. As we look back, tranquil and composed once more, upon all that we have seen, we feel that we can never hope to look upon such imposing pageantry again.

There can never be another Durbar upon the same unparalleled scale. If it is asked "Why?" the answer is ready: Because no one can ever hope to organise an Assemblage that will rival it. No future Administration can expect to excel it, and when the futility of emulation is recognised, there will be no attempt to do so. Besides, such a gathering could not, for many reasons, come oftener than once in half a century or so; and it could never assume quite the same form again, because India is rapidly changing in many respects. The old picturesque characteristics are dying hard, but they are disappearing for all that. The Maharajahs may be still willing to ride in golden howdahs upon stately elephants, but they are buying motor-cars. They still appear on ceremonial occasions clad in silks and ablaze with jewels, but they prefer you to see them on the polo ground in the garb of Tautz. Mediæval India, which gave much of the character and the colour to the functions that have just concluded, will soon be mediæval no longer. And because the old order changeth, there will never be another Durbar like this.

There is one other reason that may be adduced in support of this contention. India, let us hope, is destined to be ruled by great Viceroys in the future as in the past; but it is unlikely that she will ever have again a Viceroy so largely endowed with the qualities necessary to organise and carry to a triumphant issue such a vast celebration. It has needed a combination of the historic imagination, of supreme insight into the essentials of scenic display, of firm and tenacious determination to overcome all obstacles and convince by swift argument all opposition, of immense capacity for hard work and of a faculty for organisation which did not overlook the smallest detail. All these qualities Lord Curzon possesses in unbounded measure, and he has exercised them unsparingly. First and last, the Assemblage is the result of his own personal work. He it was who conceived it, and he alone rendered it possible of execution. His project has emerged successfully from the midst of a thousand lugubrious predictions of failure. No one, except perhaps a few political officers, will ever know how much he laboured for it. In the midst of current work that would have crushed a weaker man, he found time to consider and settle its minutest points. Nothing was too small to escape his discerning attention. Four times last year he visited Delhi to inspect the preparations, and in every branch he altered, revised, improved. It was an almost superhuman undertaking, the sort of thing that most men would have regarded as giving them reputation enough to last a lifetime; yet it is only an incident of his Viceroyalty, and the Viceroyalty is only one phase of his career. There is probably only one other living man who could have grappled with the task with the same thoroughness and the same brilliant success; and that other man is the German Emperor.

During the last day or two, those of us who are left in camp have been discussing the question:— "Which was the finest scene of the whole Assemblage?" There seems to be an absolute unanimity about the answer. Every one agrees that for spectacular display nothing equalled the Durbar. It contained more truly dramatic moments, it was conceived upon a vaster scale than any other function. That wonderful hour before the audience took their seats, when the arena was filled with a glittering throng; the moment when the Herald drew up before the dais, and his trumpeters sounded a flourish on their silver trumpets: the picture at the instant the Viceroy rose to address the gathering; and that last happy touch, when the Duke and Duchess turned and bowed to the audience amid uproarious cheers, are all unforgettable. More memorable than these recollections, because more truly tinged with pathos, is the entry of the aged veterans who had fought for the Queen in the Mutiny upon that very spot. That was the most splendid incident of the whole fortnight, by universal consent. Many a strong man was moved to tears at that touching sight. Of the indoor spectacles, the State Ball was incomparably the best; and the lovely vision of the marble halls of the Dewan-i-Khas, its jewelled precincts radiant with light, will remain fadeless. The Investiture was impressive, but too prolonged; it should have been curtailed. The scene at the State Entry, when the long line of elephants with gold and silver howdahs was approaching the Jumma Musjid, was perhaps the most remarkable embodiment of purely Oriental display that was seen; while for truly barbaric splendour, for unsuspected revelations of colour, the assembly on the plain outside the Amphitheatre, before the review of the chiefs' retinues began, undoubtedly bears the palm. One other picture stands out prominently in the mind. It is that of the sea of upturned faces, the crowds swarming on the roads and roofs and balconies, when the first showers of golden rain lit up the dark spaces around the greatest mosque in the world.

But when all has been said that can be said about the Delhi gathering—and no pen will ever describe it adequately—there will still remain the stern moralist who will ask:—"What good has it all done? We have read glowing descriptions until we are sick of them. But was it worth the expense? Will it have any lasting effect?" Well, these are difficult questions to answer, but an answer must be given to them. I think a very large proportion of the people—at any rate the English people—who came to the Durbar, came in a rather scoffing spirit; and I think, further, that very few of them are inclined to scoff now. They know what they have seen; and I fancy the dominant feeling now is that it was worth it all. You needed to have been in the midst of it to realise all that it has meant. I would say, first, that it has deepened the sense of the real permanence of British rule in India. If that had been its only result it would have been a great gain. Hitherto the people of India, taken in bulk, have never entirely accepted as a permanent reality the rule of the British. They have regarded us as fleeting eidolons, destined to disappear as their previous rulers have one after the other disappeared. The vast Imperial Assemblage, the concourse of great administrators, the grim array of armed warriors, have shown them a deeper truth. They have been the outward symbols of a solid and enduring Administration, based upon justice and tolerance, but supported by invincible strength. And when the people of India finally divest themselves of the idea that the British are mere birds of passage, their own progress towards a higher civilisation will receive an immense stimulus, because of the modification it will produce in their attitude towards schemes of reform. Again, the Durbar has done something to impress the world without with the strength and magnitude of British power in India; and that also is pure gain. For a brief space the eyes of the whole world have been turned towards Imperial Delhi. The interest may have been momentary, but it lasted long enough to convince Europe and America that this was no sham spectacle, organised out of unrealities, but was a true and vivid demonstration that the final process of welding the whole Indian Empire together under a British Emperor had been accomplished. That particular impression will not lightly fade; and though the attacks upon "decadent" England may not diminish, there will remain at the back of the minds of Continental critics the consciousness that at Delhi, in the midst of pageantry the like of which Asia has never known, an India united for the first time in history has joyfully acclaimed the accession of King Edward the Seventh. That knowledge will have due weight when next the war-clouds arise.

"But these," it may be argued, "are considerations that affect the British Empire as a whole, rather than the people of India. What has the Durbar done for them?" This question, too, must be faced and answered. I leave out of account the Viceroy's reference to the large sums that the Assemblage has put into the pockets of hundred of thousands of poor men all over the country, though it is pertinent to the issue. If money has been spent, it has been spent in India. I leave out of account, moreover, the Art Exhibition, because I do not conceive that that interesting collection will be of great permanent benefit to the industrial arts of the country. But when these aspects are dismissed, much remains. It is impossible not to believe that great good has been accomplished by the constant mingling of all the most prominent native rulers and statesmen in India during the last fortnight. People who were only names to them became visible personalities. Intercourse has been smoothed, new friendships have been made. Moreover, some rulers who were wont in their isolation to magnify their own importance, have learned their own limitations as they never knew them before. This has been peculiarly the case with the chiefs from the remoter States, and the notables from the frontiers. They confessed themselves—some of them—awed by the magnitude of the gathering, by the multiplicity of great men confronting them. They will go back to their homes with a new and deepening sense of the vast resources of the Empire. They will be less ready in future to relapse into truculence. And so, out of this Imperial Assemblage, it may be hoped that peace and concord and amity will flow in increasing measure. But far beyond this, and of the largest importance to the people of India, will be the new sense of unity which the Durbar has fostered. They have realised in very truth that they are, for the first time in many centuries, bound together in a political organisation centring in a common head. Congresses have held aloft in vain the dream of an United India; and while their demagogues have ranted and raved, the British Raj has done this thing. It has shown the people that they are really united, and it has shown them where the true bonds of unity lie. In willing loyalty to the British Crown, in mutual striving towards one common end beneath the ægis of a rule that makes for freedom and tolerance and order, that is the way of political salvation. And who shall say what new hopes and aspirations, what fresh and inspiring vistas of progress towards a higher level, this new sense of kinship may not evoke? If it helps forward the fruition of these things, the Durbar will not have been held in vain. "India a Nation," may well have been its watchword, far more than that of any Congress.

And what of England? Has the Durbar at Delhi no message and no lesson for the ancient democracy that has been intently contemplating it from afar? Surely this, told in the resounding cheers with which the King-Emperor's name was always greeted, with which the representatives of the Royal Family were always hailed: that the greatest hold which England exercises over India is the affection and veneration in which these Oriental peoples, strong in their recognition of the rights of kingship, hold the British Throne. The English race will have missed the real significance of the Durbar if they do not understand that the maintenance of the Monarchy is essential to the retention of India. If the Monarchy were to disappear—which God forbid—India would speedily slip from our grasp. The people of India must have a personal ruler endowed with the divine prerogative. One felt it when one marked the intense fervour with which every Maharajah spoke of the King-Emperor, with which every tumultuous throng acclaimed his Majesty's name. It is an extraordinary and almost unnoticed consequence of British rule in India, but it is an undoubted fact, that the possession of India has made monarchical rule more essential than ever to the English race. If we lose India, the Empire is lost. And the people of England have not realised the one great lesson of the Delhi Durbar if they do not understand that the maintenance of British rule in India, and therefore the preservation of the whole Empire, is bound up with the preservation of the Monarchy.

XXII.

THE PALACE OF DREAMS.

AGRA, *January* 18.

YOU are standing at dead of night before a mighty gateway. Its vast arch soars upward into the darkness. Its doors are closed against you. Presently the stillness is broken by a shuffling footstep within. A bolt clanks in its socket, and a little wicket gate slowly swings ajar. You enter, and find yourself in a huge demi-vault. The yellow flame of a flickering lantern hardly serves to pierce the gloom. The lofty roof is dim and remote. The light flings gigantic shadows on the walls. Two or three vague sleeping forms lie in the recesses. An air of hushed mystery envelops the place.

You pass, slow and hesitating, through the ultimate portal. In a moment the black night engulfs you again. The air is laden with the scent of trees. Dark umbrageous shapes arise. You are aware of a spacious garden. Far ahead is a glimmering pin-point of light. It is barely visible, but it serves to guide your faltering tread. And it brings a welcome suggestion of human presence in the midst of the uncanny obscurity ; for the brooding quiet of the garden is almost oppressive. There is no sound save the echo of your own footsteps, ringing along the silent grove. As you draw near, a single quivering gleam reveals an unsuspected stretch of water. Then there rises up before you the ghostly outline of a white terrace, and beyond, towering heavenward, a great pearl-grey building, misty and faint and wan.

It seems almost desecration to set foot upon the unsullied expanse of white marble that leads to the threshold of the dim shrine of the dead. You pause, unconsciously irresolute, to gaze upwards at the immense embayed entrance. Within, a few steps bring you to the loveliest sanctuary that ever man conceived. In its centre are two cenotaphs, enclosed by a delicate trellis work of marble. And as you pass through the opening in the fragile screen, and stand beside the tombs, the lantern discloses to your amazed vision that the marble is everywhere inlaid with exquisite designs in precious stones. Tomb and tracery, and even the very walls, are jewelled. Agate and jasper and cornelian, bloodstone and turquoise and lapis-lazuli, shine before your eyes, cunningly embedded in the gleaming stone. And yet, so matchless is the conception, so perfect the work, that the dominant impression is that of rich and chaste simplicity ; you never lose the sense of calm purity the marble imparts. Seen by the poor beams of a single lantern, the interior is an eerie place. Its shimmering whiteness fades away into impenetrable shadows. It is haunted by unearthly sounds. You cannot see the mighty dome, but out of its profundity there floats down to you the murmur of innumerable voices. You breathe an awe-struck whisper. Instantly the sound is caught up on high, and echoed, and reverberated, and repeated through infinite cadences, until it slowly dies away in the gloom. It is as though you were listening through the open doorway of a cathedral to a vast congregation joining in prayer. Anon it is like the despairing wail of a multitude of lost souls. There is no echo in the world so solemn and so awful. The lantern-bearer at your side raises his voice and utters a long sweet note. The glorious sepulchre is filled with liquid resonant intonations, melting into one another in a perfect diapason. It is the melody of architecture, more wondrous than the music of an organ.

You wander out upon the remotest terrace. Far below flows the river, dark and mysterious; in the distance a few lamps shine in the sleeping city. A chill wind sighs amid the trees. The solitude of the spot is profound. But it is lighter now. Soft starlight suffuses the scene. High above a flanking minaret Sirius is flaming brightly; Orion glitters beyond the dome, and the "sweet Pleiades." The cupolas of the little mosque on the right are at last clear-cut, for the sky behind them is changing from deep purple to silvery blue. From beyond the river comes the sound of voices chanting in unison. And slowly, very slowly, the amber moon arises.

Only then is the real magic and the witchery of the fabric fully revealed. The moonlight bathes it in mild radiance. Shadows deepen in its broad recesses, and throw the line of the arches into gentle relief. The pearl-grey is being transformed into opal. There is nothing hard about it yet, nothing material; the note of reticence is not yet lost. And its ethereal beauty casts upon you an irresistible spell, for it seems a promise of eternal peace, it proffers the guerdon of an unending calm. But come now along this leafy avenue. Gaze through this break in the foliage. Surely the whole world ends where the dark lawn is edged by three mournful cypresses. That cloud-like pile beyond, with its fairy turrets and its lily walls, is not of this earth. It is a thing of unsubstantiality, a relucent and diaphanous phantom transfigured in the tender light. You are peering through the branches at a ravishing glimpse of the unknown, a palace of dreams.

Lastly, go where a high marble dais is reared in the midst of the pleasaunce. Around you are stretches of moonlit water. Only the splash of a rising fish breaks the silence. An abiding serenity settles upon the scene. The moon is climbing high in the heavens. It shines with chastened splendour upon dome and cupola, its beams creep slowly across the stately entrance and transmute it afresh from opal to ivory. The sentinel minarets, half-concealed by the trees, become essential to the picture; they are in perfect harmony. The glamour seizes you like the spell of an enchantress. You fear to speak, almost to breathe, lest the charm be broken and the airy apparition dissolve. You feel that the memory of that glorious vision of luminous dome-crowned marble, with its setting of imperturbable trees and lambent pools, will haunt you to your dying day. You think no more of the dispraise of the little men who would measure it by rule of thumb, and balance it by this and that, and test it by their petty formularies. You only know that for you, upon that night of nights, it suffices. Conceived in poignant anguish, built of blood and tears, it is as though its inspired creator had by a miracle caught and embodied one of the fleeting glimpses of the unattainable unveiled at rare moments to poor humanity in the mire. And yet, even as you contemplate it entranced, you learn again the tormenting futility of mortal aspiration. The cold Pole Star poised high above it is fixed, immutable, unchanging. But the gracious palace is hardening, materialising. The unrelenting white moonlight waxes stronger; the hall of a dream grows clear and tangible and earthly. Let us remain no longer. Let us never see it in the blinding glare of noontide, or even in the flush of twilight. Rather let us cherish for ever the remembrance of that wondrous pile of opalescence beneath the rising moon, and never look upon the Taj again.

APPENDIX A.

BY THE KING-EMPEROR.

A PROCLAMATION.

FOR APPOINTING A DAY FOR THE CELEBRATION IN HIS MAJESTY'S INDIAN DOMINIONS OF THE SOLEMNITY OF THE CORONATION OF HIS MAJESTY.

EDWARD, R. I.

Whereas, upon the death of our late Sovereign of happy memory, Queen Victoria, upon the 22nd day of January in the year of Our Lord one thousand nine hundred and one, we did ascend the Throne under the style and title of Edward VII, by the Grace of God, King of the United Kingdom of Great Britain and Ireland, Defender of the Faith, Emperor of India ;

And whereas, by Our Royal Proclamations bearing date the twenty-sixth day of June and the tenth day of December in the year of Our Lord one thousand nine hundred and one, in the First year of Our Reign, We did publish and declare Our Royal intention, by the favour and Blessing of Almighty God, to celebrate the Solemnity of Our Royal Coronation upon the twenty-sixth day of June, one thousand nine hundred and two ;

And whereas, by the Favour and Blessing of Almighty God, We were enabled to celebrate the said Solemnity upon Saturday, the ninth of August last ;

And whereas, it is Our wish and desire that the fact of the celebration of the said Solemnity should be publicly announced to all Our loving Subjects within Our Indian Dominions, an opportunity should be given to Our Governors, Lieutenant-Governors, and Heads of Administrations, to the Chief Princes, Chiefs, and Nobles of the Native States under Our Protection, and to the Representatives of all the Provinces of Our Indian Empire, to take part in the said ceremonial;

Now We do, by this Our Royal Proclamation, make announcement thereof, and We do hereby charge and command Our right trusty and well beloved Councillor, George Nathaniel, Lord Curzon of Kedleston, Our Viceroy and Governor-General of India, to hold at Delhi on the 1st of January, one thousand nine hundred and three, an Imperial Durbar for the purpose of declaring the completion of the said Solemnity of our Coronation; and We direct that at the said Durbar this Proclamation shall be read for the information of all whom it may concern.

Given at Our Court at St. James's, the first day of October, one thousand nine hundred and two, in the second year of Our Reign.

GOD SAVE THE KING-EMPEROR.

APPENDIX B.

THE VICEROY'S DURBAR SPEECH.

At the Proclamation Durbar the VICEROY said :—Five months ago in London His Majesty King Edward VII, King of England and Emperor of India, was invested with the crown and sceptre of the English Kings. Only a few representatives of the Indian Empire had the good fortune to be present at that ceremony. To-day His Majesty has by his royal favour afforded an opportunity to all his Indian people to take part in similar rejoicings, and here, and elsewhere throughout India, are gathered together in honour of the event the Princes and Chiefs and Nobles, who are the pillars of his throne, the European and Indian officials who conduct his administration with an integrity and devotion to duty beyond compare, the Army, British and Native, which with such pre-eminent bravery defends his frontiers and fights his wars, and the vast body of the loyal inhabitants of India of all races who, amid a thousand varieties of circumstance and feeling and custom, are united in their spontaneous allegiance to the Imperial Crown. It was with the special object of thus solemnising his Coronation in India that His Majesty commanded me, as his Viceroy, to convene this great Durbar, and it is to signify the supreme value that he attaches to the occasion that he has honoured us by deputing his own brother, His Royal Highness the Duke of Connaught, to join in this celebration.

It is 26 years since, on the anniversary of this day, in this city of Imperial memories and traditions, and on this very spot, Queen Victoria was proclaimed the first Empress of India. That act was a vindication of her profound interest in her Indian subjects, and of the accomplished unity of her Indian dominions under the paramountcy of the British Crown. To-day, a quarter of a century later, that Empire is not less but more united. The sovereign to whom we are met to render homage is not less dear to his Indian people, for they have seen his features, and heard his voice. He has succeeded to a throne not only the most illustrious, but the most stable in the world; and ill-informed would be the critic who would deny that not the least of the bases of its security—nay, I think, a principal condition of its strength—is the possession of the Indian Empire, and the faithful attachment and service of His Majesty's Indian people. Rich in her ancient traditions, India is also rich in the loyalty which has been kindled anew in her by the West. Amid the crowd of noble suitors who, through all the centuries, have sought her hand, she has given it only to the one who has also gained her trust.

Nowhere else in the world would such a spectacle be possible as that which we witness here to-day. I do not speak of this great and imposing Assemblage, unparalleled as I believe it to be. I refer to that which this gathering symbolises, and those to whose feelings it gives expression. Over 100 rulers of separate States, whose united population amounts to 60 millions of people, and whose territories extend over 55 degrees of longitude, have come here to testify their allegiance to their common Sovereign. We greatly esteem the sentiments of loyalty that have brought them to Delhi from such great distances, and often at considerable sacrifice ; and I shall presently be honoured by receiving from their own lips their message of personal congratulation to the King. The officers and soldiers present are drawn from a force in India of nearly 230,000 men, whose pride it is that they are the King's Army. The leaders of Indian society, official and unofficial, who are here, are the mouthpieces of a community of over 230 million souls. In spirit, therefore, and one may almost say, through their rulers and deputies, in person, there is represented in this arena nearly one-fifth of the entire human race. All are animated by a single feeling, and all bow before a single throne. And should it be asked how it is that any one sentiment can draw together these vast and scattered forces and make them one, the answer is that loyalty to the sovereign is synonymous with confidence in the equity and benignity of his rule. It is not merely the expression of an emotion, but the record of an experience and the declaration of a belief. For to the majority of these millions the King's Government has given freedom from invasion and anarchy ; to others it has guaranteed their rights and privileges ; to others it opens ever widening avenues of honourable employment ; to the masses it dispenses mercy in the hour of suffering ; and to all it endeavours to give equal justice, immunity from oppression, and the blessings of enlightenment and peace. To have won such a dominion is a great achievement. To hold it by fair and righteous dealing is a greater. To weld it by prudent statesmanship into a single and compact whole will be and is the greatest of all.

Such are the ideas and aims that are embodied in the summoning of this Coronation Durbar. It is now my duty to read to you the gracious Message which His Majesty has desired me to convey to his Indian people :—

"It gives me much pleasure to send a Message of greeting to my Indian people, on the solemn occasion when they are celebrating my Coronation. Only a small number of the Indian Princes and representatives were able to be present at the Ceremony which took place in London ; and I accordingly instructed my Viceroy and Governor-General to hold a great Durbar at Delhi, in order to afford an opportunity to all the Indian Princes, Chiefs, and Peoples, and to the Officials of my Government, to commemorate this auspicious event. Ever since my visit to India in 1875, I have regarded that Country and its Peoples with deep affection : and I am conscious of their earnest and loyal devotion to my House and Throne. During recent years many evidences of their attachment have reached me : and my Indian Troops have rendered conspicuous services in the Wars and Victories of my Empire.

"I confidently hope that my beloved Son, the Prince of Wales, and the Princess of Wales, may before long be able to make themselves personally acquainted with India, a country which I have always desired that they should see, and which they are equally anxious to visit. Gladly would I have come to India upon this eventful occasion myself had this been found possible. I have, however, sent my dear Brother, the Duke of Connaught, who is already so well known in India, in order that my Family may be represented at the Ceremony held to celebrate my Coronation.

"My desire, since I succeeded to the Throne of my revered Mother, the late Queen Victoria, the First Empress of India, has been to maintain unimpaired the same principles of humane and equitable Administration which secured for her in so wonderful a degree the veneration and affection of her Indian Subjects. To all my Feudatories and Subjects throughout India, I renew the assurance of my regard for their liberties, of respect for their dignities and rights, of interest in their advancement, and of devotion to their welfare, which are the supreme aim and object of my rule, and which, under the blessing of Almighty God, will lead to the increasing prosperity of my Indian Empire, and the greater happiness of its People."

Princes and Peoples of India, these are the words of the Sovereign whose Coronation we are assembled to celebrate. They provide a stimulus and an inspiration to the officers who serve him, and they breathe the lessons of magnanimity and goodwill to all. To those of us who, like my colleagues and myself, are the direct instruments of His Majesty's Government, they suggest the spirit that should guide our conduct and infuse our Administration. Never was there a time when we were more desirous that that Administration should be characterised by generosity and leniency. Those who have suffered much deserve much; and those who have wrought well deserve well. The Princes of India have offered us their soldiers and their own swords in the recent campaigns of the Empire; and in other struggles, such as those against drought and famine, they have conducted themselves with equal gallantry and credit. It is difficult to give to them more than they already enjoy, and impossible to add to a security whose inviolability is beyond dispute. Nevertheless, it has been a pleasure to us to propose that Government shall cease to exact any interest for a period of three years upon all loans that have been made or guaranteed by the Government of India to Native States in connection with the last famine; and we hope that this benefaction may be acceptable to those to whom it is offered. Other and more numerous classes there are in this great country to whom we would gladly extend, and to whom we hope before long to be in a position to announce, relief. In the midst of a financial year it is not always expedient to make announcements, or easy to frame calculations. If, however, the present conditions continue, and if, as we have good reason to believe, we have entered upon a period of prosperity in Indian finance, then I trust that these early years of His Majesty's reign may not pass by without the Government of India being able to demonstrate their feelings of sympathy and regard for the Indian population by measures of financial relief, which their patient and loyal conduct in years of depression and distress renders it especially gratifying to me to contemplate. I need not now refer to other acts of consideration or favour which we have associated with the present occasion, since they are recorded elsewhere. But it is my privilege to make the announcement to the officers of the Army that henceforward the name of the Indian Staff Corps will cease to exist, and that they will belong to the single and homogenous Indian Army of the King.

Princes and Peoples, if we turn our gaze for a moment to the future, a great development appears with little doubt to lie before this country. There is no

Indian problem, be it of population or education or labour or subsistence, which it is not in the power of statesmanship to solve. The solution of many is even now proceeding before our eyes. If the combined arms of Great Britain and India can secure continued peace upon our borders, if unity prevails within them, between princes and people, between European and Indian, and between rulers and ruled, and if the seasons fail not in their bounty, then nothing can arrest the march of progress. The India of the future will, under Providence, not be an India of diminishing plenty, of empty prospect, or of justifiable discontent ; but one of expanding industry, of awakened faculties, of increasing prosperity, and of more widely-distributed comfort and wealth. I have faith in the conscience and the purpose of my own country ; and I believe in the almost illimitable capacities of this. But under no other conditions can this future be realised than the unchallenged supremacy of the paramount power, and under no other controlling authority is this capable of being maintained, than that of the British Crown.

And now I will bring these remarks to a close. It is my earnest hope that this great assemblage may long be remembered by the peoples of India as having brought them into contact at a moment of great solemnity with the personality and the sentiments of their Sovereign. I hope that its memories will be those of happiness and rejoicing, and that the reign of King Edward VII, so auspiciously begun, will live in the annals of India and in the hearts of its people. We pray that, under the blessing of the Almighty Ruler of the Universe, his sovereignty and power may last for long years, that the well-being of his subjects may grow from day to day, that the administration of his officers may be stamped with wisdom and virtue, and that the security and beneficence of his dominion may endure for ever. Long live the King, Emperor of India!

APPENDIX C.

THE STATE BANQUET.

At the State Banquet on January 1st, His Excellency the Viceroy entertained His Royal Highness the Duke of Connaught and a large and distinguished company. His Excellency, in proposing the toast of the King-Emperor, spoke as follows :—

YOUR ROYAL HIGHNESSES, YOUR EXCELLENCIES, MY LORDS, AND GENTLEMEN,—I rise to propose the health of His Majesty the King, Emperor of India. This afternoon we carried through, I hope with success (cheers), the great ceremony that had been devised for the celebration of His Majesty's Coronation in this country, and the spectacle was one that must have stirred the heart of every beholder. (Cheers.) It brought home to every European or Indian inhabitant of this land the vivid reality of the Constitution under which we live, and by which a far away and invisible mainspring guides with resistless energy and power every movement of this vast political machine; and I hope that it may also have impressed our various illustrious visitors and guests with the conviction that this Indian possession of His Majesty is no mere dead-weight tied on to the heels of the British Empire, but a Dominion, a Continent, an Empire by itself, rich in its own personality and memories, self-confident in its own strength, and aglow with abundant potentialities for the future. (Loud cheers.) To be King of the United Kingdom and of the British

Possessions beyond the Seas is a great and noble title. But to be Emperor of India is in no respect less, and is in some respects greater. (Cheers.) For powerful Empires existed and flourished here, while Englishmen were still wandering painted in the woods, and when the British Colonies were wilderness and jungle ; and India has left a deeper mark upon the history, the philosophy, and the religion of mankind than any other territorial unit in the universe. (Cheers.) That a British Sovereign should in the fulness of time have been able to do what no predecessor of his ever accomplished, what Alexander never dreamed of, what Akbar never performed, namely, to pacify, unify, and consolidate this great mass into a single homogenous whole, is, in my judgment, the most impressive phenomenon in history, and the greatest wonder of the modern world. (Cheers.)

Your Royal Highnesses, Your Excellencies, and Gentlemen, I venture to say that but one regret has filled all our minds here to-day. It is that His Majesty the King-Emperor has not been able to be present here in person to receive the homage of his loyal Feudatories, and the acclamations of his Indian people. (Cheers.) There is, indeed, no necessity for an Emperor of India to come out here to be crowned. His Majesty was our acknowledged and sovereign Lord as soon as the Throne was vacant-nearly two years ago. But India would dearly have loved to see the face of her Emperor and to listen to his voice : and some day we may hope that, as time and distance continue to dwindle under the magic finger of science, it may be found possible for the Viceroy on some future occasion like the present to be eliminated as a superfluous phantom (laughter), and for the real figure to appear upon the scene. (Cheers.)

However that may be, we are met here in honour of a Sovereign who, though he may be absent in person, is with us in spirit, and whose Royal Message, which I had the privilege of reading this afternoon, shows how proud he is of the allegiance, and how devoted to the interests, of his Indian people. (Cheers.) At the Durbar it was my duty to address more particularly the various classes of His Majesty's Feudatories and subjects who had assembled to render him their homage and to listen to his words. But the presence at this table here to-night of so many illustrious representatives of Foreign Powers and of eminent persons from all quarters of the globe, enables me to point to the fact that the possession of India draws with it other and outside responsibilities, and brings us into relation, I am glad to say, peaceful and amicable relation, with all the Powers and Principalities of the East. We are honoured here by the company of a distinguished representative of the great and allied Empire of Japan (loud cheers), and by an Envoy from that enlightened monarch the King of Siam (cheers); and at our Durbar there were present to-day the Envoys or representatives of our friend and ally the Amir of Afghanistan (cheers), of the friendly Kingdom of Nepal, and of the Sultan of Muscat. Among our guests are the Governors-General of the Indian possessions of two powerful and allied nations, France and Portugal, with whom our relations are those of unbroken peacefulness and concord. (Cheers.) Further, there have appeared for the first time at a gathering such as this, representatives of those great British Colonies beyond the seas, Australia and South Africa, whose star is destined to rise ever higher and higher, and whose Governments, as time passes on, must be brought into still closer connection with our own. (Cheers.) Finally, we have here prominent Members of the Imperial Legislature, of the British Lords and Commons, who have journeyed across the ocean to join hands with us in this great ceremonial. (Applause.) I think I am entitled, therefore, to claim that it is no mere local celebration, but a great and Imperial solemnity of far-reaching interest and application, that we have been enacting to-day, and it is before an audience that is typical of all that is best in the British Empire, of our established dominion in Asia, of the friendly sentiments of our neighbours, and of the sympathetic regard of our own kith and kin across the seas, that I now propose my toast. (Loud cheers.)

I give you all, Gentlemen, with feelings of profound respect, of devotion, and of enthusiasm, the health of His Majesty the King, Emperor of India. (Loud and continued cheers.)

The toast was drunk with all honours.

The Viceroy then rose to propose the health of His Royal Highness the Duke of Connaught. His Excellency said :—

YOUR ROYAL HIGHNESSES, YOUR EXCELLENCIES, MY LORDS, AND GENTLEMEN,—There is only one other toast that I shall present to you this evening. I said just now how greatly His Majesty the King-Emperor had regretted that he could not be present here in person at the celebration of his own Coronation. But as this was impossible, His Majesty took the one step that, had there been a plebiscite on the subject in India, we should all have voted for unanimously (loud applause)—namely, he deputed a member of the Royal Family, a near relative of his own, to represent his family on this occasion ;

and—the Prince and Princess of Wales finding it impossible to visit India in the present winter, though we hope that that is an honour only for a little while delayed—His Majesty's choice fell upon his Royal brother, the Duke of Connaught (loud cheers), whose presence at the ceremony to-day, and here again to-night, is regarded by all of us with quite exceptional pleasure and delight. (Cheers.) These are our feelings, both because we regard His Royal Highness's visit as testifying in the most unmistakable way to the attitude and interest of the Sovereign, and also because there is no Prince, I might go further and say, no officer—for after all His Royal Highness has been one of ourselves, and has served the Crown in India (cheers)—who has more endeared himself to the people of all classes in this country, to soldiers and civilians, to Europeans and Natives, than His Royal Highness the Duke of Connaught. (Loud cheers.) He comes back to us, therefore, not merely as the delegate of our illustrious Sovereign, but as the old friend whom all India reveres and loves (cheers); and, if I may be permitted to diverge for one moment from the strict track of my toast, I would add that these sentiments on our part are enhanced by the knowledge that His Royal Highness has brought with him the gracious Princess whose popularity in India is not second even to his own. May I also say, though it is not perhaps absolutely germane to my toast, with what pleasure we see here another member of the Royal Family, His Royal Highness the Grand Duke of Hesse, himself a reigning sovereign, and a grandson of our late Queen, who has honoured us by joining our company, and whose presence is a compliment and a delight to us all. (Loud cheers.)

And now, to revert to the subject of my toast: I hope that His Royal Highness the Duke of Connaught will carry away to His Majesty the King a favourable impression of the prosperity and loyalty of his great Indian dominion. I can assure him that we regard it as the highest honour that he should have come out to be with us on this momentous occasion. (Cheers.) When our Delhi functions are over, we hope to arrange for him a pleasant tour through the scenes and among the people to whom he is so much attached; and when he sails away from our shores, I hope that India will always keep the firm and agreeable resting-place in his memory that the Duchess and he already occupy, and will by their present visit confirm, in the affections of Europeans and Indians alike in this country. (Loud cheers.)

Gentlemen, I ask you to join with me in drinking the good health, pleasant journey, and safe return of our illustrious guest, His Royal Highness the Duke of Connaught. (Loud applause.)

The toast was drunk with enthusiasm.

His Royal Highness, who, on rising to respond to the toast, was very warmly received, said :—

YOUR EXCELLENCIES, YOUR ROYAL HIGHNESS, MY LORDS, AND GENTLEMEN,—I am indeed very sensible of the very kind manner in which you have proposed my health on this great and auspicious day. I can assure you that it was a great pleasure and satisfaction to myself when His Majesty the King informed me that it was his wish to send me out to India for the Coronation Durbar to represent his own family. (Cheers.) I never expected that I should have such good fortune. My soldiering days now are cast in a very different climate. Ireland is a very different place from India, and Dublin is a very different place from Delhi (laughter), and I was never more astonished than I was on being told that I should come out to India again. It is a great pleasure to me to come—a pleasure to come again to a country to which anybody at all interested and having served the Crown in it, must feel deeply attached.

There is also the feeling—I must say a somewhat sorrowful one—that when I was here before I had the good fortune to serve under three Viceroys and two Commanders-in-Chief, and that now I am no longer connected with India, except in my heart. (Loud cheers.) But I think it requires very little assurance from me that I do, and always shall, take the very deepest interest in everything that affects the happiness and prosperity and the greatness of His Majesty's Indian Empire. (Cheers.)

I have many friends here, both British and Native (cheers), and to see them again—to see them well and getting on in the world, is a great satisfaction to me; and what especially gives me pleasure is to meet the Native Army once again. (Cheers.) As you know, Sir, I was first connected with the Bengal Army, as it was then in this Command—the Meerut Division—and with that of the Rawalpindi Division, and then for nearly four years I had the Command of the Bombay Army, and, therefore, I may say that my interests are Indian, and not confined to one Presidency or another. But, during the twelve years that I have been in India, the whole of the forces have taken their share in the defence of our frontiers and of our interest both in India and beyond the seas, and I am happy to think that whether it was in South Africa, whether it was in China, or whether it was on the frontiers of India, every branch of the Indian Army has known how to maintain its reputation, for which I can say with confidence that the Indian Army is respected by the armies of all other nations. (Loud cheers.) It is a bad day for any Army when it does not get the chance of active service, and it would be especially so for the Indian Army if they were to be locked up year after year. However, this is a slight digression from the toast. May I be allowed to say for the Duchess of Connaught that she, equally with myself, rejoices to be again in India, and that she was very proud to be present at the ceremony of to-day ; and may I also, with reference to Your Excellency's remarks about my nephew, say how highly he appreciates the pleasure of visiting India and of being your guest, and further may I, on this New Year's Day, tell you, Lord Curzon, how grateful we all are for your great hospitality and for the very kind and cordial welcome you have given us.

I thank you all, Gentlemen, for the kind manner in which you have drunk my health. (Loud cheers.)

APPENDIX D.

THE ART EXHIBITION.

The Viceroy's speech at the opening of the Art Exhibition was as follows:—YOUR ROYAL HIGHNESSES, YOUR HIGHNESSES, LADIES AND GENTLEMEN,—It is now my pleasant duty to proceed to the first of the functions of the present fortnight, and to declare open the Delhi Art Exhibition. A good many of our visitors would scarcely believe that almost everything that we see before us, except the trees, is the creation of the last eight months. When I came here in April last to select the site, there was not a trace of this great building, of these terraces, and of all the amenities that we now see around. They have all sprung into existence for the sake of this Exhibition, and though the effects of the Exhibition will, I hope, not be so quickly wiped out, the *mise-en-scène* is, I am sorry to say, destined to disappear.

Perhaps you will expect me to say a few words about the circumstances in which this Exhibition started into being. Ever since I have been in India I have made a careful study of the art industries and handicrafts of this country, once so famous and beautiful, and I have lamented, as many others have done, their progressive deterioration and decline. When it was settled that we were to hold this great gathering at Delhi, at which there would be assembled representatives of every Province and State in India, Indian Princes and Chiefs and Nobles, high officials, Native gentlemen, and visitors from all parts of the globe, it struck me that here at last was the long-sought opportunity of doing something to resuscitate these threatened handicrafts, to show to the world of what India is still capable, and, if possible, to arrest the process of decay. I accordingly sent for Dr. Watt, and I appointed him my right hand for the purpose. Far and wide throughout India have he and his Assistant, Mr. Percy Brown, proceeded, travelling thousands of miles, everywhere interviewing the artisans, selecting specimens, giving orders, where necessary supplying models, and advancing money to those who needed it. Three conditions I laid down to be observed like the laws of the Medes and Persians.

First, I stipulated that this must be an Arts Exhibition and nothing else. We could easily have given you a wonderful show illustrating the industrial and economic development of India. Dr. Watt has such an exhibition, and a very good one too, at Calcutta. We could have shown you timbers, and minerals, and raw stuffs, and hides, and manufactured articles, to any extent that you pleased. It would all have been very satisfying, but also very ugly. But I did not want that. I did not mean this to be an industrial or economic Exhibition. I meant it to be an Arts Exhibition, and that only.

My second condition was that I would not have anything European or quasi-European in it. I declined to admit any of those horrible objects, such as lamps on gorgeous pedestals, coloured glass lustres, or fantastic statuettes, that find such a surprising vogue among certain classes in this country, but that are bad anywhere in the world, and worst of all in India, which has an art of its own. I laid down that I wanted only the work that represented the ideas, the traditions, the instincts, and the beliefs of the people. It is possible that a few articles that do not answer to my definition may have crept in, because the process of Europeanisation is going on apace in this country, and the number of teapots, cream jugs, napkin rings, salt cellars and cigarette cases that the Indian artisan is called upon to turn out is appalling. But, generally speaking, my condition has been observed.

Then my third condition was that I would only have the best. I did not want cheap cottons and wax-cloths, vulgar lacquer, trinkets and tinsel, brass gods and bowls made to order for Birmingham or perhaps made in Birmingham itself. What I desired was an exhibition of all that is rare, characteristic, or beautiful in Indian art, our gold and silver ware, our metal work and enamels and jewellery, our carving in wood and ivory and stone, our best pottery and tiles, our carpets of old Oriental patterns, our muslins and silks and embroideries, and the incomparable Indian brocades. All of these you will see inside this building. But please remember it is not a bazaar: but an exhibition. Our object has been to encourage and revive good work, not to satisfy the requirements of the thinly-lined purse.

Such is the general character of the Exhibition. But we have added to it something much more important. Conscious that taste is declining and that many of our modern models are debased and bad, we have endeavoured to set up alongside the products of the present the standards and samples of the past. This is the meaning of the Loan Collection, which has a hall to itself, in which you will see many beautiful specimens of old Indian art ware, lent to us by the generosity of Indian Chiefs and connoisseurs, some of it coming from our own Indian Museums, and some from the unrivalled collection in the South Kensington Museum in London. Many of these objects are beautiful in themselves : but we hope that the Indian workmen who are here, and also the patrons who employ them, will study them not merely as objects of antiquarian or even artistic interest, but as supplying them with fresh or rather resuscitated ideas which may be useful to them in inspiring their own work in the future. For this may be laid down as a truism, that Indian art will never be revived by borrowing foreign ideals, but only by fidelity to its own.

And now I may be asked, What is the object of this Exhibition, and what good do I expect to result from it? I will answer in a very few words. In so far as the decline of the Indian arts represents the ascendancy of commercialism, the superiority of steam power to hand power, the triumph of the test of utility over that of taste, then I have not much hope. We are witnessing in India only one aspect of a process that is going on throughout the world, that has long ago extinguished the old manual industries of England, and that is rapidly extinguishing those of China and Japan. Nothing can stop it. The power loom will drive out the hand loom, and the factory will get the better of the workshop, just as surely as the steam car is superseding the horsed carriage, and as the hand-pulled punkah is being replaced by the electric fan. All that is inevitable, and in an age which wants things cheap, and does not mind their being ugly, which cares a good deal for comfort, and not much for beauty, and which is never happy unless it is deserting its own models and traditions, and running about in quest of something foreign and strange, we may be certain that a great many of the old arts and handicrafts are doomed.

There is another symptom that to my mind is even more ominous. I am one of those, as I have said, who believe that no national art is capable of continued existence unless it satisfies the ideals, and expresses the wants, of the nation that has produced it. No art can be kept alive by globe-trotters or curio-hunters alone. If it has got to that point, it becomes a mere mechanical reproduction of certain fashionable patterns: and when fashion changes, and they cease to be popular, it dies. If Indian art, therefore, is to continue to flourish, or is to be revived, it can only be if the Indian Chiefs and aristocracy, and people of culture and high degree, undertake to patronise it. So long as they prefer to fill their palaces with flaming Brussels carpets, with Tottenham Court Road furniture, with cheap Italian mosaics, with French oleographs, with Austrian lustres, and with German tissues and cheap brocades, I fear there is not much hope. I speak in no terms of reproach, because I think that in England we are just as bad in our pursuit of anything that takes our fancy in foreign lands. But I do say that if Indian arts and handicrafts are to be kept alive, it can never be by outside patronage alone. It can only be because they find a market within the country and express the ideas and culture of its people. I should like to see a movement spring up among the Indian Chiefs and nobility for the expurgation, or at any rate the purification, of modern tastes, and for a reversion to the old-fashioned but exquisite styles and patterns of their own country. Some day I have not a doubt that it will come. But it may then be too late.

If these are the omens, what then is the aim of this Exhibition, and what purpose do I think that it will serve? I can answer in a word. The Exhibition is intended as an object lesson. It is meant to show what India can still imagine, and create, and do. It is meant to show that the artistic sense is not dead among its workmen, but that all they want is a little stimulus and encouragement. It is meant to show that for the beautification of an Indian house or the furniture of an Indian home, there is no need to rush to the European shops at Calcutta or Bombay, but that in almost every Indian State and Province, in most Indian towns, and in many Indian villages, there still survives the art, and there still exist the artificers, who can satisfy the artistic, as well as the utilitarian, tastes of their countrymen, and who are competent to keep alive this precious inheritance that we have received from the past. It is with this object that Dr. Watt and I have laboured in creating this Exhibition; and in now declaring it open, it only remains for me to express the earnest hope that it may in some measure fulfil the strictly patriotic purpose for which it has been designed.

APPENDIX E.

THE WORKERS.

One undischarged duty still devolves upon the chronicler of the Durbar festivities at Delhi. It is that of noting briefly the work of some of the men who toiled early and late for months together to make the gigantic gathering a success. To appreciate the extent of their labours, it is necessary to convey some idea of the vast magnitude of the camp; and despite all that has been written about it, one fears that no adequate conception of its size has been gathered by those who did not see it. The actual work of preparation on the ground itself took over a year.

The share Lord Curzon took in these manifold labours has been explained on a previous occasion. This letter deals only with the services of some of his many lieutenants. First among these comes Sir Hugh Barnes, who on the evening of the Investiture received the phenomenal honour of knighthood in two orders within an hour. Sir Hugh Barnes was the President of the Central Committee, and had the chief executive responsibility of the whole gathering. He had to attend to innumerable details of all kinds, and with unfailing good humour and calmness coped with an amount of work which would have killed a less capable man. For months he undertook the control of the preparations in addition to his normal duties at the Foreign Office; but latterly he was compelled to hand over the Foreign Secretaryship to Mr. Dane. All the arrangements for the Durbar and the Investiture, all the minute points of precedence these functions presented for settlement, were in his charge. Yet even at the moments when he was most overwhelmed, he never lost patience or tact; and no one can say that they ever saw him in the least degree flurried. Sir Hugh Barnes, acting on the sound principle of choosing as helpers men whose worth you have personally proved, selected as his principal A.-D.-C. Mr. R. Hughes-Buller, who had worked with him in former years in Baluchistan. Mr. Hughes-Buller was thereby brought into a prominence at all the principal functions, second only to that of Sir Hugh himself; and it may be said of this member of a Department not too well supplied just now with men of such exceptional attainments, that his energy and tact and boundless capacity for work made an impression almost equal to that created by his distinguished chief. Another official of the Foreign Office who played a considerable part, particularly at the State Investiture, was the Under-Secretary, Mr. J. B. Wood, who was entrusted with the difficult task of handling much of the ceremonial procedure, which he accomplished with notable skill. Every province sent a special attaché to relieve the Foreign Office of the duty of meeting the ruling chiefs on their arrival. These special attachés were also told off to assist at the official gatherings, and had a large amount of hard and not very agreeable work to do. Some of them will not soon forget the way in which the vagaries of the railways compelled them to wait about draughty stations in the bitter cold, sometimes for the greater part of the night, to receive chiefs whose trains were lost in the outer darkness. One other official of the Foreign Office who undertook unusually exacting duties was Mr. O. V. Bosanquet, who was placed in charge of the Press and Consular Camp. The residents in his camp owe him a debt of gratitude for his great courtesy and consideration, and his unwearying kindness in ministering to their wants. Some idea of his zealous labours may be gathered from the fact that he did not permit himself to leave the camp to attend a single public gathering. On the last day of the festivities Mr. Bosanquet was entertained by the representatives of the Press at a dinner, and was asked to accept a silver bowl as a token of regard.

Another important member of the Central Committee was Major-General G. Henry, who was responsible for laying out the military camps, and for organising the great commissariat depôts; he was ably assisted by Major H. Hudson, I.S.C., who held a post on the small Executive Committee. The work done by these two officers did not come very much before the public, but it was extremely valuable. Then there was Mr. T. Gordon Walker, I.C.S., with his assistant, Major M. W. Douglas, the local Deputy Commissioner, who jointly represented the Punjab Government in the work of preparation. It fell to their lot to select the camping sites, to arrange for the compensation of cultivators, to make provision for supplying water for the various camps, and to attend to the many other details with which the Punjab Administration was specially concerned. Major Douglas also had to supervise the erection of the stands for the public in the city of Delhi. Lieutenant-Colonel Baring, the Viceroy's Military Secretary, was also a member of the Central Committee. How Colonel Baring found time to attend to the many tasks imposed upon him must remain a mystery. He was the principal organiser of the Polo Tournaments ; he was expected to keep an eye on the chief Visitors' Camp (No. 1) and on the Viceroy's Camp ; he had to look after the requirements of the distinguished guests from home ; and he had further to discharge his ordinary duty of supervising the official hospitality of the Viceroy. He not only survived the ordeal, but emerged from it with triumphant success. It should be noted that Captain J. Pinney, of the Central India Horse, was in personal charge of the Polo Tournaments, for which he laboured long and arduously. A notable functionary was Captain A. D. Bannerman, the Secretary of the Executive Committee, whose manifold duties included the laying out of the civil camps, a task necessitating exceptional tact. Mr. F. S. Cowie, I.C.S., was the Secretary of the Central Committee, and among other things was responsible for the preparation of the elaborate Camp Directory.

Colonel J. W. Thurburn, R.E., was in charge of the engineering arrangements of all the camps, while Rai Bahadur Ganga Ram acted as Superintendent of Works. Ganga Ram had to attend to innumerable undertakings. The construction of the water-supply ; the preparation and maintenance of fifty miles of roads ; the building of the Amphitheatre and the Viceroy's House ; the enlargement of the Diwan-i-Am and Diwan-i-Khas ; all these works, and many others, fell to his special lot. Few people expected that he would complete them in time. Only a fortnight before the Durbar, predictions of unreadiness were still prevalent. But Ganga Ram confounded his critics, for everything was in order on the appointed day. The decoration of the temporary additions to the Diwan-i-Khas, and the adornment of the ceiling, were the work of that talented craftsman, Bairam Singh, who decorated the Indian room at Osborne for the late Queen-Empress. The artistic additions to the Diwan-i-Am were in charge of Bhoota Singh. And here, perhaps, it may be mentioned that the internal arrangements for the State Investiture and the State Ball were in the hands of Major Berger, A.-D.-C., and Captain Bateman-Champain, of the 1st Gurkhas. The latter officer, who controlled the seating arrangements at the Investiture, had to work day and night owing to the late date at which the extension of the Diwan-i-Am was completed.

One admirable feature of the Central Camp was the excellent installation of the electric light. The wiring of the tents was a matter requiring very delicate handling; yet from the day early in December when the light was first switched on, it never failed for an instant. Messrs. Kilburn and Co., of Calcutta, erected the plant, which consisted of 100 arc and 8,000 incandescent lamps; and the installation was supervised by Major Stuart, R.E., and Captain Halliday, R.E. Another satisfactory characteristic of the Assemblage was the noteworthy absence of any serious outbreak of sickness, and for this somewhat unexpected result ample credit is due to Lieutenant-Colonel Bamber, I.M.S., the Sanitary Commissioner of the Punjab, to Lieutenant-Colonel Thornhill, the Executive Sanitary Officer, and to their numerous assistants, for the careful precautions they devised. Whatever may be thought of the railway arrangements on the trunk lines, the little Durbar Light Railway, which was constructed and directed by Captain R. A. L. Hepper, R.E., was a distinct success, and proved a useful adjunct to the camp. The work of the big railways is so much a matter of controversy that it will hardly bear discussion, but perhaps sufficient allowance has not been made by the public for the extraordinary pressure produced by the rush to Delhi. On the East Indian Railway, Mr. Murray, the District Traffic Superintendent, did good work until his health gave way under the heavy strain; and after his departure Mr. Peddie filled his place with conspicuous devotion. There is every reason to fear that the lamented death of Mr. Liever, the Executive Engineer of the line, was directly due to the stress of his labours. On the North-Western Railway, Mr. C. J. Keene, the Deputy Traffic Superintendent, is of all overworked railway officials the one most worthy of mention.

The transition from railways to telegraphs is natural, and the work of Mr. F. G. Maclean, the Director-General of Telegraphs, deserves special acknowledgment. Mr. Maclean not only opened eleven temporary telegraph offices at different camps, for the receipt of private telegrams, but he had to tackle an amount of press work such as the Indian Telegraph Department has never before had to deal with. I can only say that I never heard a single complaint that any Press message, either to an Indian address or to England, did not reach its destination in ample time. The arrangements for delivering private messages in camp, on the other hand, were anything but good; but it must be recognized that the conditions presented unusual difficulties and the public frequently accentuated the muddle by faulty addresses. Of the postal arrangements, which were in charge of Mr. C. Stewart Wilson, Postmaster-General of the Punjab, and of Rai Daulat

Ram Bahadur, nothing but good can be spoken. Collections and deliveries alike were carried out with singular promptitude and accuracy.

There are many other officials who deserve special recognition, but space only permits the bare mention of a few of their names. The exertions of Sir George Watt, with his assistants, Mr. Percy Brown and Mr. Cecil Burns, in connection with the Art Exhibition, have been alluded to on a previous occasion. Lieutenant-Colonel Lyons-Montgomery, of the Executive Committee, organised a Central Supply and Transport Market which was of the utmost value to the camp. Mr. P. Bramley, a D. S. P. from the United Provinces with a special knowledge of elephants, rendered valuable aid in marshalling the mighty beasts that figured so largely in the State entry. Khan Saheb Mohamed Hassan, the Secretary of the Jumma Masjid Committee, was constant in his efforts to afford full facilities for the spectators who witnessed the State entry and the fireworks from the great mosque. An officer with a real genius for directing military music was discovered in Captain Sanford, of the Punjab Commission, who had charge of the musical arrangements. Major Dunlop-Smith, with Major C. F. Minchin and Captain E. Barnes, organised the review of native Chiefs' retinues, the most picturesque of all the functions of the Assemblage. Mr. W. E. Jardine, an eminent civilian, had charge of the ticket arrangements, and became the most pestered official in camp in consequence. His lot for the last fortnight before the Durbar was anything but happy, and his mail bags were packed with applications every day. Mr. Brown, Inspector-General of Police, Punjab, was in charge of the Police arrangements, which were exceptionally efficient. The list might be continued indefinitely. Rarely has so much loyal and laborious service been given in connection with a single gathering. One other name, however, will occur to most of those who were present in camp. It is that of the Viceroy's Private Secretary, whose devoted and incessant labours can only be guessed at in view of his constant self-effacement. All who know him rejoiced on New Year's morning at the announcement of his new dignity.—*Times of India*, January 23.